Jama

Don Philpott

Florida

Gulf of Mexico

Bahamas

Florida Keys

Great Bahama Bank

JAMAICA

Cuba

N
W E
S

ATLANTIC OCEAN

Cayman Islands

JAMAICA

Kingston

Haiti

Dominican Republic

CARIBBEAN SEA

Dedication

To Pam, my beautiful American Rose.

Acknowledgements

My thanks to everyone who assisted me in the writing of this guidebook.
In particular, I would like to thank the Jamaican Tourist Board,
the Sandals team, Jorge Martinez and Barrington Edwards.

JAMAICA

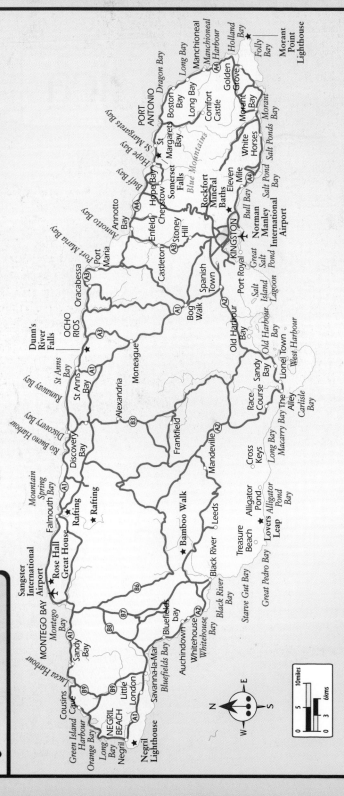

Jamaica

Don Philpott

CONTENTS

• FEATURE BOXES •

*I*ntroduction

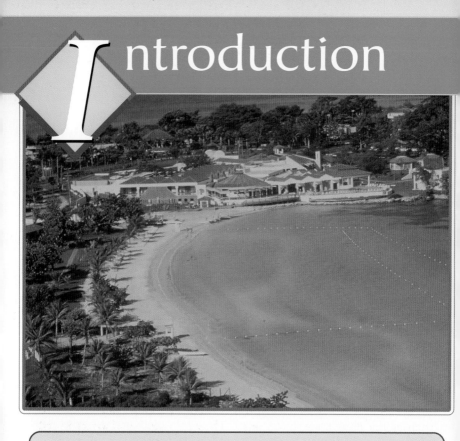

Jamaica is a fabulous year-round holiday destination with stunning natural beauty and a wealth of attractions and recreational opportunities. There are superb palm-fringed, golden sand beaches, secluded coves, warm, turquoise seas, superb scenery, historic landmarks and world-class diving, fishing and sailing. There is a huge range of accommodation from luxury resorts to charming, homely, welcoming guesthouses, great food, rum and reggae and a welcome everywhere that is as warm as the Jamaican sun.

The perfect place to have fun

GEOGRAPHY

Jamaica is the third largest of the Caribbean islands and the largest of the English-speaking islands. It is 90 miles (145km) south of Cuba, and 390 miles (628km) north east of Cape Gracias a Dios in Nicaragua, the nearest point on the American continent.

The island was formed as a result of massive volcanic activity about 140 million years ago, when it was literally heaved up from the floor of the sea. Between 40 and 50 million years ago the land mass was again submerged, and about 15 to 20 million years ago, the East Pacific and Caribbean plates broke apart and the upheaval produced huge ridges such as the Blue Mountains, and massive depressions, like the 24,750ft (8,120m) deep Cayman Trench to the west of Jamaica. The edge of the East Caribbean plate then slid under the edge of the American plate, and was tilted, which thrust many of the mountain peaks upwards creating a chain of islands, including Jamaica.

The limestone that constitutes most of the island is the result of millions of years of sedimentation and compression of dead marine life on the sea bed. Cockpit Country is an area of limestone particularly susceptible to water erosion. This erosion process has resulted in the incredible landscape of caves, gorges and strangely-shaped limestone hillocks.

The island covers 4,411 sq miles (11,424 sq km), and is 146 miles (235km) long and between 22 and 51 miles (35 and 82km) wide. It consists of coastal plains with an interior of limestone mountains and plateau, increasing in altitude as they run from west to east. It is very mountainous with almost half the island more than 1,000ft (305m) above sea level. Blue Mountain Peak is the highest point at 7,402ft (2,256m). There are about 120 rivers, and those in the north tend to be shorter and run faster than those in the south, where many of the waterways have formed fertile alluvial plains. The Black River runs for 44 miles (71km) to the sea in the south west, it is the island's longest river and navigable by small boat for 25 miles (40km) from its estuary. There are a number of waterfalls and mineral springs, four of which have bathing facilities.

Tides vary little around the island, and the difference between high and low tide is rarely more than 16in (41cm).

HISTORY

The island's first settlers were Amerindians from South America. They paddled their way north in open canoes about 5000BC. Their descendants the peaceful Arawaks arrived between AD600 and AD700, and established settlements throughout the island. They were farmers and fishermen who lived in small villages ruled by chiefs called caciques. The Arawaks named the island Xaymaca, which means 'land of wood and water', and the name has changed only slightly over the centuries to become Jamaica.

When Columbus 'discovered' Jamaica on 5 May 1494, during his second voyage, his ships were met by about 70 Arawak canoes. The Arawaks were overawed by the Spaniards, their ships and weapons, and treated them as gods. There were about 100,000 Arawaks on the island, and many were later enslaved.

Columbus

Columbus landed at what is now Discovery Bay, and called the island Santiago. After a few days he sailed west past what is now Montego Bay, which he named Golfo de Buen Tiempo. In his log he wrote: 'it is the fairest isle that my eyes have beheld.... the mountains touch the sky', and in recognition of the discovery, the Spanish King granted Santiago to the Columbus family.

Columbus spent almost a year stranded on the island between 1503 and 1504 during his fourth voyage, after two of his three worm-eaten ships sank in St Anns Bay. Two members of his crew paddled a canoe to Hispaniola to alert the authorities and have replacement ships sent.

In 1509 the first European settlement was founded by Juan de Esquiva at Sevilla la Nueva on the north coast close to St Ann.

The first African slaves were introduced about 1517. The settlement did not prosper because of the unhealthy climate and disease, and in 1534 it was moved to what became Villa de la Vega, later called Santiago de la Vega (St Jago de la Vega), and finally Spanish Town. Plantations reared cattle and grew staple foods to feed the island, the settlements on Hispaniola and passing Spanish ships. Archaeological excavations have started to unearth Sevilla la Nueva.

THE ARRIVAL OF THE SPANISH

The Spanish and in particular their Western diseases, proved disastrous for the Arawaks. Many were taken away as slaves to work in the gold and silver mines on Hispaniola, and by the end of the sixteenth century, almost all had died in slavery or from disease. Although the Arawaks disappeared, however, there are many reminders of their culture and language. Words such as tobacco, hurricane, hammock, potato, maize, barbecue, cannibal and canoe, all come from the Arawak language.

At the beginning of the seventeenth century, the island had a population of about 3,000 Spanish and a few African slaves. The Spanish invested in Jamaica at first because they thought there was gold, but when none was found, they lost interest and did little to develop Jamaica. During the first half of the seventeenth century, there were frequent raids on Jamaica by English and French forces. It was also frequently attacked by pirates, but it remained in Spanish hands.

In May 1655, a British force led by Admiral William Penn landed off what is now Kingston and captured

Jamaica with hardly a fight. Most of the Spanish, alerted to their imminent arrival, had fled to the north of the island then escaped by boat to Cuba. The Spanish attempted to recapture the island in June 1658 but were defeated in a major battle at Rio Nuevo. Spanish troops fled to the mountains and were not finally expelled until 1660.

ARRIVAL OF THE BRITISH

The British take-over signaled a period of rapid expansion as British planters arrived and the island became virtually one huge sugar cane plantation, earning enormous profits. In London at the time, a frequently heard expression was 'as rich as a West Indian planter'. Thousands of slaves from West Africa, particularly the Fanti, Ashanti, Ibo and Yoruba tribes were shipped across in chains to work the plantations.

Many of the slaves of the Spanish fled to the mountains, resisting all attempts at capture. These former slaves were called Maroons, from the Spanish word cimarron meaning 'wild', and their numbers were swelled by runaway British slaves. They lived in fortresses in the mountains, and eventually to end the fighting, the British signed peace treaties with them in 1739-40, granting the Maroons effective self-government over their mountain territories. Descendents of the Maroons still live in the parish of Trelawny, in the hilly Cockpit Country and in the mountains at Moore Town.

Privateers and Pirates

Jamaica was under military rule until 1661 when Edward D'Oyley was appointed the first British Governor. Largely with official approval, Jamaica became the base for many privateers and pirates who preyed on the rich Spanish treasure galleons sailing the Spanish Main. The British authorities not only turned a blind eye on these activities, but secretly encouraged them as the British and Spanish were frequently in dispute, and all the time privateers were harassing Spanish vessels and tying up the Spanish navy, the British did not need to have a naval fleet stationed on Jamaica.

Port Royal became the base for many of the Caribbean's most famous and infamous pirates, such as Henry Morgan, and later Bristol's Edward Leach, known as Blackbeard, and Calico Jack with his female crew.

The Treaty of Madrid in 1670 recognized Britain's title to the island, and in 1672 the Royal African Company was founded with a monopoly of the English slave trade. Jamaica became one of the largest slave markets in the world, and although the pirates had largely been driven out, the island became a hub for smugglers trading with Spanish America. Jamaica rapidly prospered and was one of the most valuable of all the British colonial possessions with 70 sugar mills, 60 indigo factories and 60 cocoa mills. The wealth of the island was such that in 1678 the British Crown tried to levy its own royal taxes. When the island's legislature refused to accept this, its privileges were revoked and it was not until 1682 that they were restored. It was not until 1728 that the issue was resolved when the island agreed to pay the Crown £6,000 a year in lieu of the uncollected royal taxes, in return for an undertaking that new taxation had to be approved by the island's legislature.

Port Royal was largely destroyed by an earthquake in 1692 and the site chosen for the new capital became Kingston. Shortly after the earthquake a Spanish force invaded Jamaica taking advantage of the disarray, but the attackers were defeated at Carlisle Bay. Jamaica's prosperity was boosted even further in 1713 by the Treaty of Utrecht which gave Britain the right to supply slaves to all the Spanish West Indies possessions.

The island continued to prosper and in 1739 there were more than 400 sugar plantations on the island, and more than 5,000 slaves, although this was only a fraction of the Africans sold in the Jamaica slave markets and shipped to other Caribbean islands. In 1760 there was an unsuccessful slave uprising led by Tacky, one of many against the harsh conditions most had to endure.

FRENCH INTERVENTION

A bid by France and Spain to seize control of Jamaica in April 1782 failed when their combined fleets were defeated by a British naval force, led by Admiral Rodney, at the Battle of the Saints off Dominica. It was the most decisive British victory ever in the Caribbean, and had the battle gone the other way, Britain could well have lost all its West Indian colonies.

Another attempt by the French to take Jamaica in 1806 was defeated by Admiral Sir John Duckworth. At this time Jamaica had more than 30,000 slaves working on the hugely profitable sugar cane and coffee plantations. The last slave uprising was in Montego Bay over Christmas, 1831, and led by Baptist preacher Sam Sharpe, and although unsuccessful, it paved the way for Emancipation two years later.

Freedom from Slavery

All slaves were granted their freedom by the British Government in 1834, but in effect they did not get their freedom until 1838. Following protests from the plantation owners alarmed at the sudden loss of cheap labor, it was agreed that all slaves serve a four-year apprenticeship before finally being given their freedom. They had to agree to work free of charge for their old masters for three-quarters of each working week, but were allowed to spend any other time working their own plots of land cleared from the forest.

After emancipation and 'apprenticeship', large numbers of freed slaves left the plantations and moved to the hills, clearing the land to establish their own 'free villages'. These settlements, like Wilberforce, named after the anti-slavery campaigner, and Seaford, resulted in most of the inland villages and communities that can be seen today. The owners received £19 for each slave freed, but with a shortage of labor, many of the plantations ceased to be profitable.

Above left: Ocho Rios
Above Right: Franklyn D. Resort
Below: Cranbrook, with Cranbrook orchids in the foreground

Indian and Chinese labor was introduced and the railroad was built to help ease transport, but the island's decline continued. Widespread poverty and unemployment led to an uprising in Morant Bay in October, 1865, led by a black Baptist deacon called Paul Bogle in which a magistrate and 18 white residents were killed. The uprising was harshly put down and hundreds of people including Bogle were publicly executed. Although not involved in the uprising Kingston legislator G. W. Gordon, who had spoken in defense of the poor was also tried and publicly hanged.

RECALL OF GOVERNOR

The savagery of the authority's response led to the recall of Governor Eyre, and the abolition of the island's legislature, with all power effectively transferred to the new Crown Colony Governor, Sir John Peter Grant. He introduced a judicial system, public health, education, police, government savings bank and a public works department. He oversaw the introduction of irrigation and the planting of the first bananas, the island's 'green gold'. His administration saw a recovery in the island's fortune, and in 1872 the capital was moved from Spanish Town to Kingston. In 1887 national hero Marcus Garvey was born in St Anns Bay, and he was largely instrumental in laying the roots for Rastafarianism (see St Annes Bay).

On 14 January 1907 the island was hit by a major earthquake, and about 800 people were killed. Most of the buildings in Kingston and Port Royal were destroyed or badly damaged in the earthquake or the fire that then swept through the towns. Kingston's impressive present

Emigration

The island has seen major emigration over the last 150 years. The 1850s saw the first wave of emigration from the island with many Jamaicans moving to Panama as railroad workers. There was a second wave in the late 1870s as the French sought workers to help build a canal across the Isthmus of Panama. Although this project failed many Jamaicans moved to Panama in the early 1900s to work on the construction of the US funded Panama Canal, while others were employed on the sugar cane and coffee plantations in Cuba, and the banana plantations of Central America.

There was also significant emigration from Jamaica to the US from the end of the nineteenth century until quotas were introduced. Canada then became the focus of emigration and eventually Britain in the 1950s. During the decade about 200,000 Jamaicans emigrated to the UK until quotas were introduced. Since the mid-1960s most emigration has been to the US and Canada. This emigration has led to a situation whereby more Jamaicans live outside the country than within it.

layout is largely as a result of rebuilding following this disaster.

The island has had representative government since 1884, and powerful trade unions and political parties emerged after rioting in 1938 brought about by the harsh economic conditions following the

Depression. The People's National Party was founded by Norman Manley (PNP), and the Jamaican Labour Party (JLP), was founded by Manley's cousin Alexander Bustamante. A new constitution in 1944 introduced a house of representatives elected by universal suffrage, and full internal government was obtained in 1959, although external policy was still determined by Britain. Jamaica attained full independence on 6 August, 1962, with Queen Elizabeth II the head of state, represented on the island by the Governor-General. General elections are often violent affairs and best avoided. The two major political parties are still the JLP and the ruling PNP, led by the Rt. Hon Percival J. Patterson who was appointed Prime Minister in 1992 on becoming the new party leader.

PEOPLE

The vast majority of the 2.6 million population are descended from African slaves, although there is a multi-racial mix. Apart from African and Afro-Europeans, there are East Indians, Indians, Chinese and Afro-Chinese, descendents of workers who came to the island as indentured labor. There are also small groups of European descent, predominantly English but also German, Portuguese and Lebanese. The island has a very young age profile with about two-thirds of the 800,000 plus residents of Kingston under the age of 30. English is the official language but a local Creole patois is widely spoken.

The vast majority of Jamaicans take their religion very seriously, and many are members of indigenous religious groups such as Pocomania and Revivalism, which believe that spirits roam the earth, and Rastafari, which gave birth to the island's distinctive national music called reggae, popularized world-wide by the late Bob Marley.

There are also a number of cults that combine aspects of Christianity with West African traditions, folklore and tribal religions, such as Bongo and Kumina which involves rhythmic dancing and drumming.

The Government has expanded its successful 'Meet the People' project, which gives visitors the opportunity

Rastafarianism

There is no doubt that Rastafarianism is largely misunderstood, partly perhaps because of the appearance of many of its adherents who, for religious reasons, wear their hair in dreadlocks. Rastafarians are generally young, peace-loving, teetotal vegetarians, who worship the Black Messiah. Their spiritual leader is the late Emperor Haile Selassie of Ethiopia, whom they believe is still with them, and whose title includes 'ras' meaning prince and 'tafari' meaning 'to be feared'. They believe they are one of the lost tribes of Israel and that Ethiopia is the Promised Land. They do not smoke tobacco but many use 'sacred' ganja, which they smoke from a pipe called a chalice, which reinforces the religious symbolism attached to it. Most prefer to commune with nature and avoid the tourist areas, but there are many Rasta imitators who try to hustle for money, so be warned.

Captain Bligh

Captain Bligh introduced breadfruit to the Caribbean in 1793. He brought 1200 breadfruit saplings from Tahiti aboard the *Providence*, and these were first planted in Jamaica and St Vincent, and then quickly spread throughout the islands. It was Bligh's attempts to bring in young breadfruit trees that led to the mutiny on the *Bounty* four years earlier. Bligh was given the command of the 215-ton *Bounty* in 1787 and was ordered to take the breadfruit trees from Tahiti to the West Indies where they were to be used to provide cheap food for the slaves.

The ship had collected its cargo and had reached Tonga when the crew, under Fletcher Christian, mutinied. The crew claimed that Bligh's regime was too tyrannical, and he and 18 members of the crew who stayed loyal to him, were cast adrift in an open boat. The cargo of breadfruit was dumped overboard. Bligh, in a remarkable feat of seamanship, navigated the boat for 3,600 miles (5796km) until making landfall on Timor in the East Indies. Some authorities have claimed that it was the breadfruit tree cargo that sparked the mutiny, as each morning the hundreds of trees in their heavy containers had to be carried on deck, and then carried down into the hold at nightfall. It might have proved just too much for the already overworked crew.

Whatever the reason for the mutiny, the breadfruit is a cheap carbohydrate-rich food, although pretty tasteless when boiled. It is best eaten fried, baked or roasted over charcoal. The slaves did not like it at first, but the tree spread and can now be found almost everywhere. It has large, dark green leaves, and the large green fruits can weigh 10 to12lbs (4.5 to 5.4kg). The falling fruits explode with a loud bang and splatter the pulpy contents over a large distance. It is said that no one goes hungry when the breadfruit is in season.

Puerto Seco Beach

Above Left: Rastafarian man
Above Left: Look no hands!
Below: Buying fresh fruit from one of the island's markets

to spend time with islanders. Volunteers in Kingston, Montego Bay, Ocho Rios, Negril, Port Antonio and other centers open their homes and lives to entertain holidaymakers in a number of ways, from being invited to dinner or a trip into the countryside, to spending a day on the beach with a family or spending time at their workplace. Details of how to participate in the program are available from Jamaica Tourist Board offices abroad or on the island.

National Symbols

Jamaica's Coat of Arms was granted in 1661 and designed by the Archbishop of Canterbury. It has remained virtually unchanged ever since, and shows a male and female Arawak standing on either side of a shield, which bears a red cross with five golden pineapples. The crest is a Jamaican crocodile surmounting the Royal Helmet and Mantlings with the motto: 'Out of Many One People'.

The national bird is the doctor bird, a humming bird found only on Jamaica, the national fruit is the ackee, an edible fruit brought to Jamaica from West Africa in the eighteenth century. The national flower is the lignum vitae (Wood of Life), which is indigenous to Jamaica, and gets its name because of medicinal qualities ascribed to it. The national tree is the blue mahoe, which has economic importance, and is popular with furniture makers because of its attractive blue-green wood that polishes well.

CULTURE

Jamaica because of its multi-racial mix has a rich cultural heritage and tradition. There is reggae whose roots are in African drum music, soca and calypso, folk dance and folk art, and above all, Carnival which brings all of these together and much more. Mento is Jamaican to its roots and can be sad and plaintive, loud and lively, or downright sexy like ska. Music is played everywhere, and usually at full volume. It blasts from open doors, from passing cars and buses, and bars seem to compete with each other for the largest and loudest speakers.

Reggae Sunsplash and Reggae Sumfest are Jamaica's two international annual reggae events. Sunsplash is held at the Bob Marley Centre in Montego Bay in late July and attracts more than 200,000 people over five days. Sumfest takes place in August also in Montego Bay, and both events attract the world's top reggae names.

Carnival is celebrated around the island after Lent, and particularly in Kingston, Montego Bay and Ocho Rios. The Negril Carnival is held in the summer. The Jamaica Cultural Development Commission organizes a series of events between March and August to showcase local talent in the performing, visual and entertainment arts. And, another popular August event is the ten-day Portland Jamboree held in Port Antonio, with street parades, parties, street dancing and cultural events. In October, the National Mento Yard takes place across the island and offers traditional and cultural folk events, arts and crafts and traditional dishes.

The Cultural Training Centre

promoted by the Institute of Jamaica, fosters art and sponsors many awards and exhibitions, and runs schools of art, dance, drama and music. The Institute is also responsible for the excellent National Library and National Gallery, and there are many other public and privately-run galleries. Jamaica has produced a wealth of acclaimed writers and artists. There are the Intuitives and Revivalists like Kapo, and the Jamaica School, a style which developed from the 1920s, which includes Edna Manley, and the new wave avant-garde. The work of contemporary artists can be seen gracing many of the island's hotels, such as the massive and spectacular wall decoration by Margaret Robson in the reception area of the Strawberry Hill Hotel in the Blue Mountains.

The Festival

The Festival is the major annual cultural event, and is now incorporated as part of the Independence celebrations at the beginning of August. There are fine art displays, arts and crafts exhibitions, cooking displays, literary, theatrical and musical events and competitions. It also includes parades and the Miss Jamaica Pageant.

There are several theatre and musical groups, and the National Dance Theatre Company, formed in 1962, is widely acclaimed and frequently performs abroad. It stages its summer season between mid-July and mid-August at the Little Theatre, New Kingston, with a second season in November and early December. It features every dance form, including traditional dances such as the quadrille, which was adapted from the European version. There is the Jamaica Philharmonic, the National Chorale, the Jamaica Folk Singers and various musical and dramatic groups at the University of the West Indies.

Another cultural tradition is the National Pantomime that opens its season on Boxing Day at the Ward Theatre in Kingston. It is a magical mix of panto tradition, and Jamaican satire, and even if you cannot understand the patois, it still makes a great night out. The Barn Theatre and the Centre Stage, both in New Kingston, also stage theatrical productions.

ECONOMY

Agriculture, mining, manufacturing and tourism are the mainstay of the island's economy. There are still some large estates but most farmers have holdings of 5 acres (2 hectares) or less. Sugar cane and bananas are the main crops, although coffee, citrus, cocoa, ginger, tobacco and pimento are grown. Smallholders still grow crops which they sell on to women called 'higglers' who sell the produce in the markets, a practice that has been carried on since before Emancipation. Fishing is a major industry although mostly for the home market.

The mountains are rich in minerals and silica for glass, ceramic clays, marble, phosphates and limestone are extracted commercially. Bauxite and refined alumina for export is the main mineral-industry, and most gypsum is also exported. Other industries produce cement, processed foods, textiles, metal products, printing and rum. Jamaica Promotions (JAMPRO) is a statutory body which encourages local and foreign investment. Tourism is increasingly important as an income earner.

Major exports are sugar cane, bananas, coffee, bauxite, alumina and clothing, although world markets for all but coffee and clothing are declining, and coffee production has only recently recovered from the damage caused by Hurricane Gilbert.

Ganja

Although illegal, ganja (marijuana) is still exported. After Emancipation, Indian indentured labor was introduced, and these workers brought with them the herb ganja. It quickly spread and was legal until the First World War. It is still largely tolerated because it has for so long been part of the island's culture, and many homes openly cultivate it in their gardens. There have been concerted efforts, however, to crack down on large-scale production that was flown out from private airstrips. Many islanders use ganja in one form or another, and it is easily available. It can be smoked, taken as a herbal tea or steeped in rum or wine which is then drunk, and most Jamaicans consider it a herb rather than a drug. Possession, however, is a serious crime and there are stiff penalties if caught with the drug.

NATURAL HISTORY

The island has a wide variety of habitats because of different vegetation zones created by the mountains, and centuries of planting. Flowers, fruit trees and plants have been imported from Africa, Asia, the Pacific, England and even evergreens from Canada.

PLANT LIFE

Originally the island was covered entirely by trees that were cleared for plantations. Today there are distinct vegetation zones. The main vegetation zones consist of lush, tropical coastline with mangrove swamps, tropical rain forest with West Indian mahogany, lignum vitae and mahoe, the national tree, and giant vines and huge stands of towering bamboo; high mountain landscapes with elfin woodlands, and near-desert cactus belts in the south. There are even tracts of rolling green land which reflect their former owners and look as if they might be parts of the English countryside – except for the palm trees.

There are wonderful flowering plants and trees such as jasmine, orchids, hibiscus, poinsettia, thryallis and bougainvillea, the amazing century plant, which blooms every ten years or so, and the spreading cotton tree, which can grow to be hundreds of years old. The cotton tree figures prominently in folklore as ghosts (duppies) are said to live among the branches. Although hibiscus and bougainvillea bloom everywhere, neither are native to the islands. Bougainvillea, named after a French explorer, was brought to the West Indies from Brazil in the early 1700s, while the hibiscus comes from Hawaii.

Banana Plantation

Jamaica has more botanical gardens than any other Caribbean island and most homes have impressive flower gardens, especially in Mandeville. The flamboyant tree with its spectacular red flowers originally came from Madagascar, while the tulip tree, which bursts into a canopy of red blossom, comes from West Africa. The frangipani, however, is a native, and one of the most spectacular flowering trees.

There are many species of palm, including the towering royal palm, the native prickly pole and macca fat, and coco palms which fringe many of the beaches. Other common tree species include West Indian cedar, ebony, Spanish elm, boxwood, red-barked turpentine, strangler fig, bay rum, sandbox, satinwood, rosewood, fiddlewood, kapok, yellow cedar, mahoe, wattle, cinnamon and buttonwood.

Many of the trees are grown for their fruit. These include the native pimento, ackee, fig, mango, guango, casuarina, almond, guava, sugar apple, soursop, coconut, tamarind and breadfruit. The seagrape, which can be found along many beaches, produces edible fruit, but is much more important because its roots prevent sand erosion.

Cacti and acacia abound in the lowland areas, and there are several species of climbing cactus which often only bloom at night.

Orchids

There are more than 235 species of orchid of which 60 species are endemic and mostly found in the hills.

It is interesting to note that the first two species of orchids ever to flower at Kew Gardens were plants shipped from Jamaica in 1787 and 1788. And, it was another Caribbean orchid that started the orchid growing craze in Europe in the nineteenth century, after being exhibited at the Great Exhibition in London's Crystal Palace.

There are also hundreds of different species of ferns and grasses, and at least 80 species of pine. The giant pea vine can be found along riverbanks smothering other vegetation in its path.

MARINE LIFE

The marine environment is even more spectacular. There are scores of species of brightly marked fish to be seen in and around the coral reefs, while the warm waters teem with larger fish, especially game fish such as tarpon, tuna, barracuda, jacks, sailfish, marlin, kingfish, swordfish and wahoo. There are also Queen conch, southern stingray, long-spined black sea urchin, and green, hawksbill, loggerhead and trunk turtles, all threatened species. The mountain mullet is the most numerous fresh water fish. Manatees can be seen grazing off the south coast. Coral is very delicate and should not be touched and never damaged or removed. Some coral, such as fire coral, needs treating with great caution, but most are beautifully marked and safe. There are more than 50 species of coral, some of which are only found off Jamaica. Most common corals include seafan, staghorn, elkhorn, brain, large star, pillar and orange reef.

Coral reefs are the ocean's equivalent to tropical rain forests, and only grow in waters with a year-round temperature of 68°F (20°C). Stony coral grows less than half an inch (1.25cm) a year, and staghorn, the fastest growing coral in the Caribbean, only grows between 4 and 6 in (10 to 15cm) a year. There are hundreds of types of shells and the inshore waters and beaches are a shell collector's dream.

Whale watching is a popular pastime from February to April as humpback whales pass by the islands on their annual migration, and there are boat trips to see them.

The Manchineel

The manchineel, which can be found on many beaches, has a number of effective defensive mechanisms that can prove very painful. Trees vary from a few ft to more than 30 ft in height, and have widely spreading, deep forked boughs with small, dark green leaves and yellow stems, and fruit like small, green apples. If you examine the leaves carefully without touching them, you will notice a small pinhead sized raised dot at the junction of leaf and leaf stalk. The apple-like fruit is poisonous, and sap from the tree causes very painful blisters, and was used as a poison. It is so toxic, that early Caribs are said to have dipped their arrow heads in it before hunting trips, and an effective, and apparently often used untraceable method of killing someone in olden times, was to add a few drops of the sap to their food over a period. The sap is released if a leaf or branch is broken, and more so after rain. Avoid contact with the tree, don't sit under it, or on a fallen branch, and do not eat the fruit. If you do get sap on your skin, run into the sea and wash it off as quickly as possible.

ANIMAL LIFE

Island wildlife includes more than 25 species of bats; fruit, insect and fish-eating, the coney, a large member of the rodent family including the Jamaican hutia, a species of hog rat; and the mongoose, which was imported in 1872 from Asia, to kill rats – which came ashore from ships – and snakes that flourished in the sugar cane plantations. The three species of snake are all harmless. The blind worm snake lives below the ground, the tree boa rarely grows to more than 1.5 ft (0.5m) in length, and the elusive Jamaican boa constrictor, which lives in the high forest, can grown up to 10 ft (3m) long – although there are stories of much longer serpents. There are many species of toads and small frogs, including the snoring frog, the world's second largest tree frog, and freshwater terrapins.

There are several species of lizards including the rare iguana, the Jamaican gecko or croaker, and anoles that puff out their throats and are able to change shade like chameleons. The galliwasp lizard is harmless although folklore claims it is poisonous. There are wild pigs in the mountains, although these are rarely seen, and the largest creatures are the endangered Jamaica crocodiles, known locally as alligators, and found on the south coast.

Some insects, especially the mosquitoes, can be a nuisance. There are wasps, ants and termites. Scorpions are very rarely seen and the trapdoor spider, which lives in a small burrow, can bite but is very timid and rarely does so.

Most insects, however, are a delight. There are more than 100 species of butterfly, many of them large and spectacular, and some swallowtails have a wing span of more than 6 in (15cm). The Islanders call butterflies 'bats', while bats are known as 'rat bats'. There are also fascinating stick insects which can grow to 10in (25cm) in length, and scores of different beetles, fireflies and dragonflies.

BIRDS

More than 250 species of birds have been recorded. Jamaica has 25 native species and it attracts migrants from both north and south America. The national bird is the indigenous streamer tail hummingbird, also known as the doctor bird, with beautifully, iridescent green plumage and long tail feathers that give it its name. There are several other species of humming bird including the mango hummingbird, and the tiny bee, or vervain hummingbird. The black and yellow sugar bird, is the 'yellow bird' in the famous calypso of the same name.

Other species include the strutting grackle which has little fear of man, the Jamaican euphonia, Blue Mountain vireo and the Jamaican tody. This is also known as the robin redbreast, although it has a white breast with a vivid red throat, and lays its eggs in a burrow underground. There are two species of parrot – green – black and yellow billed – Guiana parrotlet, wild canary, nightingale (identical to the mocking bird), solitaire, egret kingbird, the rare crested quail dove, thrush, sparrow, crow and several types of bird of prey, the most common of which is the turkey buzzard, also known as John Crow. Around the coast and out to sea, you can spot brown pelicans, the magnificent frigate bird, great blue heron, white-tailed tropicbird, gulls and terns.

**Above: Flowers of Jamaica, (left) Bougainvillea and (right) Hibiscus
Below: A great way to relax at pool side bar at Sandals**

• CLIMATE •

Average annual temperature is 82°F (27°C) although there are usually welcoming onshore breezes during the day. The daytime onshore winds are known locally as the 'doctor's breeze', while the overnight winds which come down the mountains and blow out to sea, are called the 'undertaker's breeze'.

Maximum temperatures rarely top 90°F (32°C) on the coast, or fall below 40°F (4°C) in the high mountains. Temperatures drop about 3.5°F for every 1,000 feet (305m) of altitude, so the Blue Mountain Peak has an average annual temperature of 56°F (13°C). Average annual rainfall is 78inches (198cm) with the wettest months being May and June and September and October. Rainfall varies enormously around the island, however, because of the influence of the mountains. Some high mountain areas get more than 300inches (118cm) a year, while the dry southern plains get about 30inches (12cm). Summer thunderstorms are also common and while they do not last long, they can be very heavy and give you a good soaking if caught unawares.

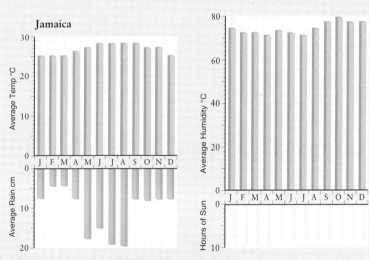

Jamaica lies in the hurricane belt although major storms are thankfully, a rare occurrence. The main hurricane season is from June to October, with August and September generally posing the greatest risk. Because of constant tracking, however, considerable warning is given of the approach of any tropical storm. If a warning is given, follow advice given locally. The area is also susceptible to earthquakes but there have only been two sizeable tremors in the last 400 years – in 1692 and 1907.

Migratory birds include many species of warblers, bobolink, buntings, king bird and large numbers of sea birds and waders.

As most of the plants, fruits, vegetables and spices will be new to the first time visitor, the following brief descriptions are offered:

FRUITS

Ackee

Ackee (akee) are hugely popular in Jamaica and the fruit is part of the national dish of salt cod and ackee. The tree is a member of the soapberry family and is a native of West Africa. It grows to about 30ft (10m) and is widely cultivated for its fruit, which is sold from road side stalls around the island. It was introduced to Jamaica by Captain Bligh, thus its botanical name of Blighia sapida. When ripe, the bright red fruit split open to reveal three segments of white flesh each with a large black seed. The soft white flesh is eaten as a vegetable and has the look and texture of pasta.

Bananas

Bananas are one of the Caribbean's most important exports, thus their nickname 'green gold' – and they grow everywhere.

There are three types of banana plant. The banana that we normally buy in supermarkets originated in Malaya and was introduced into the Caribbean in the early sixteenth century by the Spanish. The large bananas, or plantains, originally came from southern India, and are mostly used in cooking. They are often fried and served as an accompaniment to fish and meat. The third variety is the red banana, which is not grown commercially, but which can occasionally be seen around the island.

A banana produces a crop about every nine months, and each cluster of flowers grows into a hand of bananas. A bunch can contain up to twenty hands of bananas, with each hand having up to 20 individual fruit. Although they grow tall, bananas are not trees but herbaceous plants which die back each year. Once the plant has produced fruit, a shoot from the ground is cultivated to take its place, and the old plant dies.

Bananas need a lot of attention, and island farmers will tell you that there are not enough hours in a day to do everything that needs to be done. The crop needs fertilizing regularly, leaves need cutting back, and you will often see the fruit inside blue tinted plastic containers, which protect it from insect and bird attack, and speed up maturation. Jamaica is still a major exporter of bananas and shipments in 1996 are expected to top 100,000 tons.

The Bay tree

The Bay tree is from the Windward Islands, a member of the Laurel family and can grow to a height of 30 ft (10m). The leaves can be crushed for their oil which is used in the perfume industry. The leaves are used in cooking.

Calabash tree

Calabash trees are native to the Caribbean and have huge gourd like fruits that are very versatile when dried and cleaned. They can be used as water containers and bowls, bailers for boats, and as lanterns. Juice from the pulp is boiled into concentrated syrup and used to treat coughs and colds, and the fruit is said to have many other medicinal uses.

Cinnamon

Cinnamon comes from the bark of an evergreen tree, also related to the laurel. The bark is rolled into 'sticks' and dried, and then ground or sold in small pieces. It is used as a spice, and adds a sweet, aromatic taste to many dishes. Oil from the bark is added to sweets, soaps, toothpastes and liqueurs, while oil from the leaves is used in perfumes.

Cocoa

Cocoa was another important crop, and its Latin name theobroma means 'food of the gods'. A cocoa tree can produce several thousand flowers a year, but only a fraction of these will develop into seed bearing pods. It is the heavy orange pods that hang from the cocoa tree which hold the beans that contain the seeds that produce cocoa and chocolate.

The beans, containing a sweet, white sap that protects the seeds, are split open and kept in trays to ferment. This process takes up to eight days and the seeds must be kept at a regular temperature to ensure the right taste and aroma develop. The seeds are then dried. In the old days people used to walk barefoot over the beans to polish them to enhance their appearance. Today, the beans are crushed to extract cocoa butter, and the remaining powder is cocoa. Mixing cocoa powder with cocoa butter and sugar makes chocolate.

You can buy cocoa balls in the markets and village shops, which make a delicious drink. Each ball is the size of a large cherry. Simply dissolve the ball in a pan of boiling water, allow to simmer and then add sugar and milk or cream, for a rich chocolate drink. Each ball will make about four mugs of chocolate.

Coconut

Coconut palms are everywhere and should be treated with caution. They are incredibly hardy, able to grow in sand and even when regularly washed by salty sea water. They can also survive long periods without rain. Their huge leaves, up to 20ft (6m) long in mature trees, drop down during dry spells so a smaller surface area is exposed to the sun that reduces evaporation. Coconut palms can grow up to 80ft (29m) tall, and produce up to 100 seeds a year. The seeds are the second largest in the plant kingdom, and these fall when ripe.

Anyone who has heard the whoosh of a descending coconut and leapt to safety, knows how scary the sound is. Those who did not hear the whoosh, presumably did not live to tell the tale! Actually, very few people are injured by falling coconuts and that is a near miracle in view of the tens of thousands of palms all over the island, but it is not a good idea to picnic in a coconut grove!

The coconut traditionally bought in greengrocers, is the seed with its layer of coconut surrounded by a hard shell. This shell is surrounded by copra, a fibrous material, and this is covered by a large green husk. The seed and protective coverings can weigh 30lbs (13.5kg) and more. The seed and casing is waterproof, drought proof and able to float, and this explains why coconut palms which originated in the Pacific and Indian Oceans, are now found throughout the Caribbean – the seeds literally floated across the seas.

The coconut palm is extremely versatile. The leaves can be used as thatch for roofing, or cut into strips and woven into mats and baskets, while the husks yield coir, a fiber resistant to salt water and ideal for ropes and brushes and brooms. Green coconuts contain delicious thirst-quenching 'milk', and the coconut 'meat' can be eaten raw, or baked in ovens for two days before being sent to processing plants where the oil is extracted. Coconut oil is used in cooking, soaps, synthetic rubber and even in hydraulic brake fluid.

As you drive around the island, you will see groups of men and women splitting the coconuts in half with machetes preparing them for the ovens. You might also see halved coconut shells spaced out on the corrugated tin roofs of some homes. These are being dried before being sold to the copra processing plants.

Dasheen

Dasheen is one of the crops known as 'ground provisions' in the Caribbean, the others being potatoes, yams, eddo and tannia. The last two are close relatives of dasheen, and all are members of the aroid family, some of the world's oldest cultivated crops. Dasheen with its 'elephant ear' leaves, and eddo grow from a corm which when boiled thoroughly can be used like potato, and the young leaves of either can be used to make callaloo, a spinach-like soup. Both dasheen and eddo are thought to have come from China or Japan but tannia is native to the Caribbean, and its roots can be boiled, baked or fried. Callaloo is still grown in gardens and can be seen growing wild.

Coffee

Writer Ian Fleming who lived on Jamaica was a champion of the island's coffee, and his most famous character, super-spy James Bond, would only drink Blue Mountain coffee. It is considered by many to be the most aromatic coffee, and it is certainly one of the most expensive. It has less caffeine than other beans and the taste comes from the volcanic loam in which it is grown high in the Blue Mountains. The price is high because demand outstrips supply as it takes five years to harvest the first crop of cherries (beans).

Coffee was introduced to the Caribbean from the Middle East, and in 1723, Louis XV of France is said to have sent three coffee plants collected in the Yemen to Martinique. Two plants died during the voyage, and the third somehow finished up in Jamaica where it was planted, and the coffee industry was born. Coffee planting was encouraged to reduce the island's dependence on sugar, and flourished.

Most of the coffee estates were destroyed by the 1951 hurricane, and in 1973 the Government introduced the Blue Mountain appellation. Only four estates were allowed to sell 100% Blue Mountain Coffee, and the others had to label their products Blended, High Mountain Blend and Low Land Coffee. Hurricane Gilbert also hit the industry badly in 1989 although production is now back to pre-1989 levels.

Nutmeg

Nutmeg trees originally came from the Banda Islands in Indonesia and for centuries its source was kept secret because it was such a valuable commodity to the merchants selling it. In 1770 a French naturalist raided the islands, then under Dutch control, and stole several hundred plants and seedlings that were planted on Mauritius and in French Guyana, but these almost all died.

At the end of the eighteenth century Britain was at war with Napoleon Bonaparte and Holland, which had allied with France. The British captured the Banda Islands during the war and before they handed them back in 1802 as part of the Treaty of Amiens, they had learnt the secret of the nutmeg and successfully planted it in Penang in Malaya, and tropical territories around the world, including the West Indies.

The tree thrives in hilly, wet areas and the fruit is the size of a small tomato. The outer husk, or pericarp, which splits open while still on the tree, is used to make the very popular nutmeg jelly.

Guava

Guava is common throughout the island, and the aromatic, pulpy fruit is also a favorite with birds who then distribute its seeds. The fruit-bearing shrub can be seen on roadsides and in gardens, and it is used to make a wide range of products from jelly to 'cheese', a paste made by mixing the fruit with sugar. The fruit that ranges in size from a golf ball to a tennis ball, is a rich source of vitamin A and contains lots more vitamin C than citrus fruit.

Mango

Mango can be delicious if somewhat messy to eat. It originally came from India but is now grown throughout the Caribbean and found wherever there are people. Young mangoes can be stringy and unappetizing, but ripe fruit from mature trees that grow up to 50ft (18m) and higher, are usually delicious, and can be eaten raw or cooked. The juice is a great reviver in the morning, and the fruit is often used to make jams and other preserves. The wood of the mango is often used by boatbuilders.

Passion fruit

Passion fruit is not widely grown but it can usually be bought at the market. The pulpy fruit contains hundreds of tiny seeds, and many people prefer to press the fruit and drink the juice. It is also commonly used in fruit salads, sherbets and ice creams.

Pawpaw tree

Pawpaw trees are also found throughout the islands and are commonly grown in gardens. The trees are prolific fruit producers but grow so quickly that the fruit soon becomes difficult to gather. The large, juicy melon-like fruits are eaten fresh, pulped for juice or used locally to make jams, preserves and ice cream. They are rich sources of vitamins A and C. The leaves and fruit contain an enzyme which tenderizes meat, and tough joints cooked wrapped in pawpaw leaves or covered in slices of fruit, usually taste like much more expensive cuts. The same enzyme, papain, is also used in chewing gum, cosmetics, the tanning industry and, somehow, in making wool shrink-resistant. A tea made from unripe fruit is said to be good for lowering high blood pressure.

Pigeon Pea

Pigeon Peas are widely cultivated and can be found in many back gardens. The plants are very hardy and drought resistant, and give prolific yields of peas that can be eaten fresh or dried and used in soups and stews.

Pimento (allspice)

Pimento, or allspice, is a native of Jamaica and an important ingredient in many dishes. Jamaica is also the leading exporter of this spice. The dried berries are said to have the combined taste of cinnamon, clove and nutmeg, which is how it gets its name. The dried fruit is used for pickling, for curing meat and adding taste to wines, and it is usually an ingredient in curry powder. An oil extracted from the berry and leaf is used in the perfume and pharmaceutical industries.

Pineapples

Pineapples were certainly grown in the Caribbean by the time Columbus arrived, and were probably brought from South America by the Amerindians. Jamaica's native pineapple was sent to Hawaii. The fruit is slightly smaller than the Pacific pineapple, but the taste is more intense.

Sugar Cane

Sugar Cane is still grown commercially on the island. The canes can grow up to 12ft tall and after cutting, have to be crushed to extract the sugary juice. Most estates had their own sugar mill powered by water wheels or windmills. The remains of many of these mills can still be seen around the island, as well as much of the original machinery, mostly made in Britain. After extraction, the juice is boiled until the sugar crystallizes. The mixture remaining is molasses and this is used to produce rum.

Sugar Apple

Sugar Apple is a member of the anona fruit family, and grows wild and in gardens throughout the islands. The small, soft sugar apple fruit can be peeled off in strips when ripe, and is like eating thick apple sauce. It can be eaten fresh or used to make sherbet or drinks. Soursop, is a member of the same family, and its spiny fruits can be seen in hedgerows and gardens. It is eaten fresh or used for preserves, drinks and ice cream.

Turmeric

Turmeric comes from the dried root and underground stems of a plant, which is a relative of ginger. The bright yellow spice is used to add taste to foods, and as a coloring, in English mustard for instance. It is also used as a dye.

Vanilla plant

The **Vanilla plant** is a climbing member of the orchid family which produces long, dangling pods containing beans. The vanilla is extracted by distilling the beans and is used as a food flavoring, as well as in the pharmaceutical industry.

FOOD

You can dine in style enjoying international cuisines from around the world, or the best of Creole cooking. You can experiment with local vegetables and enjoy the freshest of fish and shellfish, or sample the many ethnic restaurants, from Mexican to Chinese and Lebanese to finest French. There is also a wide range of fast food outlets, both US and Jamaican-style, for those who want to eat in a hurry and get back out into the sun as quickly as possible. Remember, however, that this is still the Caribbean and there is not the same degree of urgency experienced elsewhere, so if you think things are taking a long time, order another drink, relax and take in the view.

The great attraction of Jamaican cooking is that it is a blend of so many other cuisines. Some cooking styles have been passed down from the Arawak Indians, others were introduced from Africa, India and China, there are still traces of Spanish, and you can still be offered traditional Yorkshire pudding. The overriding emphasis in all Jamaican food, however, is fresh, natural and spicy, with food purchased, prepared and served as quickly as possible.

One of the great attractions is being able to dine alfresco. Most hotels and large restaurants accept credit cards but to avoid embarrassment always check first to make sure that if you do need cash you have enough. Dining out is not only fun, it is very affordable. It seems a shame to visit Jamaica and not enjoy the excellent local spicy dishes, especially in true Jamaican eateries, which offer excellent value.

ISLAND FAST FOOD

Eating on the move or out of doors can be very enjoyable, and there are many opportunities to eat from the snack bars on the street or by the beach. This 'street food' ranges from juices and ice creams tasting of local fruits, to hot snacks such as fritters, patties and roti. Most of this food is fried but it is usually wholesome, delicious and cheap. Snacks include pork chops, conch fritters, fried pumpkin slices, and johnny cakes (unleavened fried bread).

Patties and pates, are pastry envelopes filled with seafood or spiced meat, especially beef, and rotis, which originated in the East Indies, are another form of soft pastry envelope stuffed with curried meats or vegetables. Take care if ordering a chicken roti, because in many places the meat contains small bones, which some people like to chew on!

Jamaican 'fast food' is traditionally served on a bed of rice in a take-away paper box, which makes it great for picnics.

For real fast food, stop by one of the road side stalls and buy freshly picked fruit or pick out a green coconut for a refreshing drink. The vendor will slice the top of the coconut off and make a hole so you can drink the liquid inside. When you have finished drinking, hand the coconut back, and the vendor will split the nut in half and chop off a sliver of the hard shell which you use as a spoon to gouge out the white soft jelly inside. Always ask for a really green coconut because the liquid is sweeter, and the jelly softer.

FISH AND SEAFOOD

There is wonderfully fresh seafood, especially lobster, conch, yellowfin

Firefly view

tuna, grouper and wahoo, a large mackerel type fish. Crabcakes are a specialty of the islands, as are conch fritters, and Solomon Grundy, which are delicious, seasoned, pickled herrings. Try peppered shrimps or Stamp and Go (crispy cod fritters) at one of the roadside or beachside stalls, which serve a variety of island 'fast food' specialties, like patties, pastries and fritters.

Try Caribbean black bean or red pea soup (for pea always read bean), pumpkin soup , conch chowder or callaloo, a rich soup made from spinach and kale with pieces of pepper, flakes of fish, crab and meat and often, spiced up with pepper. Pepperpot soup can be another meal in itself, made with salted meat and vegetables with local spices and seasonings.

National Dish

Jamaica's national dish is ackee and salt fish, served with hot boiled rice and buttered callaloo. Ackee, like breadfruit, was brought from Africa as a cheap food for the slaves. It is a bright yellow fruit that is usually sautéed, and then mixed with tomatoes, scallions and spices before being added to the fish. Ackee can only be picked after the pods open naturally, and must be vigorously boiled to remove a toxin that can be poisonous. When boiled and served, it looks like scrambled eggs and has the taste and texture of pasta.

Rice and peas (kidney beans) are usually served as accompaniments to main meals, although you may be offered green bananas, fried plantain, pumpkin or sweet potatoes. Cho-cho is a sort of squash, used in soups, stews or served as a vegetable.

Many fruits are also traditionally served with meats. Sweet yam is often served with fish and meat instead of potato, yellow yam is also served as a potato substitute and has a nutty taste. The ortanique is a juicy cross between a tangerine and a Seville orange, unique to Jamaica, and the cho-cho, is also boiled and served as an accompaniment to meat.

Jamaica produces some of the world's finest ginger and this is used to make cakes, puddings and the famous Old Jamaica ginger beer.

Specialty Dishes

These include jerk (Jamaican barbecue) chicken and pork, with the seasoned meat marinated for hours and then slowly cooked over a pimento wood fire in a pit in the ground. The pit is covered and the fire burns very slowly so the meat retains all its taste while becoming saturated with the taste of the wood. This method of cooking was developed by the Maroons who discovered that if the meat was cooked slowly, it was 'cured' and would keep longer. Jerk Centers, either restaurants or road side stalls, offer great food, pork, chicken, wonderful sausage and fish. The food is often impressively chopped into bite-size pieces with a machette, and the meal is served with a bammie (or bammy) or festival, savory and sweet muffin-shaped cassava rolls, and a hot pepper sauce which should be treated with the utmost caution until you have determined just how hot it is!

Escovitch fish is another island specialty, in which pieces of fish are sautéed in a peppery vinegar, lime juice and onion sauce. It can be served hot or cold, and usually comes with a bammie. Fish or vegetable run-down is a dish cooked with coconut milk, scallions and peppers.

You might be offered Souse, a delicious meat stew in which lots of unmentionable bits from the pig are used, including head and tail. There are curries which were brought to the islands by Indian laborers in the mid-nineteenth century, and are delicious. They can feature conch, chicken, lamb or goat. Another island specialty is tripe and beans.

There are wonderful fresh fruit juices, and the fruit is also used to make tasty desserts that often include soursop ice cream or sapodilla pudding. Try ortaniques, star apple, soursop, sapodilla, ugli, pineapple and mango, or fresh paw paw (papaya) sliced with a squeeze of lime juice. There are also coconut cakes, guava cheese, pastries and duckunoo, made from green bananas, coconut, cornflour, sugar and nutmeg and steamed in a banana leaf.

JAMAICAN DRINKS

YO, HO, HO AND A BOTTLE OF RUM.

Columbus is credited with planting the first sugar cane in the Caribbean, on Hispaniola, during his third voyage, and the Spanish called it aguardiente de cana, meaning cane liquor. The Latin name for sugar cane is saccharum, and it was English sailors who shortened this to rum.

The first rum was produced at least 300 years ago and became an important international commodity. It figured prominently in the infamous Triangle Trade in which slaves from Africa were sold for rum from the West Indies that was sold in Europe to raise money to buy more slaves.

Rum had such fortifying powers that General George Washington insisted every soldier be given a daily ration, and a daily tot also became a tradition in the British Royal Navy. Jamaica rum is considered the world's finest, and there are still a number of distilleries on the island producing rum using traditional methods, and most can be visited and their wares tasted and purchased. All sorts of rums are produced from light to dark and of varying strengths.

The island's most famous rum is Appleton Rum. It has been produced on the Appleton Estate since 1745, and may well have been made long before that. How the distillery started is surrounded by legend. There are stories that shipwrecked sailors came ashore at Black River in the fourteenth century, and made their way inland to the fertile Nassau Valley where sugar cane grew, and they produced the first rum. It is known, however, that the Appleton Plantation in the Black River Valley, was one of several owned by Cabel and Ezekiel Dickinson, the grandsons of one of Lord Oliver Cromwell's lieutenants, who helped capture Jamaica from the Spanish in 1655. By 1755 rum was the plantation's major product. The Estate was acquired by John Wray and his nephew in 1825. They continued the traditions of producing only the finest aged rums, a tradition that continues today.

OTHER DRINKS

Rum features in many of the island's most popular cocktails, but there are many excellent local soft drinks as well, such as mauby, sometimes maubi, made from a mixture of herbs, bark and ginger, or sorrel, made from the flowers of the plant. Red Stripe is the excellent island-brewed beer and the same brewery produces Dragon Stout, a dark beer. Beer is usually served UK-style – at room temperature. Ting, is a refreshing carbonated grapefruit drink and, of course, there is Tia Maria, flavored with Blue Mountain Coffee, and one of the world's great liqueurs.

There are also many different sorts of herbal and fruit teas available that make great thirst quenchers and revivers. Jamaican ginger, the finest in the world, led to the creation of ginger ale, and Blue Mountain Coffee is one of the world's best, and most expensive.

DRINK RECIPES

Planter's Punch

Combine 2 ounces each of pineapple juice, rum, cream of coconut and half an ounce of lime in a blender for one minute. Pour into a chilled glass, add a sprinkle of coconut shavings and garnish with a cherry and a slice of orange.

Jamaica Rum Punch

An easy way of remembering the recipe is to recall an old saying that goes: 'one of sour, two of sweet, three of strong, and four of weak'.

Mix one part lime or lemon juice, two parts of strawberry syrup, three parts of rum and four parts of water or fruit juice. Pour over crushed ice and add a slice of orange, lime, lemon or a wedge of pineapple. The punch is even better if prepared and allowed to 'mature' for 24 hours.

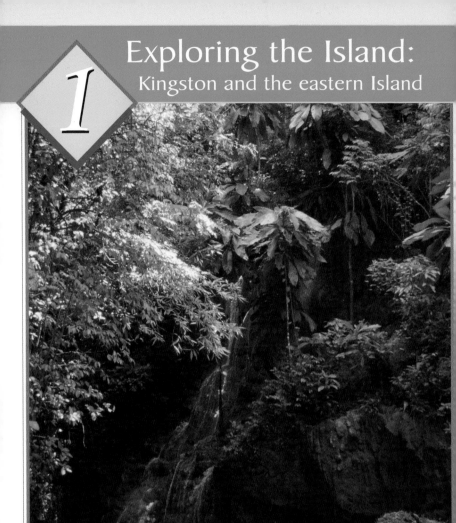

The island is divided into three counties – Cornwall, Middlesex and Surrey – and 14 parishes. These are Hanover, Westmorland, St James, Trelawny, and St Elizabeth in Cornwall; St Ann, St Mary, Manchester, Clarendon and St Catherine in Middlesex; and the combined Kingston and St Andrew Corporation, St Thomas and Portland in Surrey.

KINGSTON AND THE EASTERN TOUR

Kingston is the capital and the commercial, administrative and cultural heart of the island. It is the largest English-speaking city in the Caribbean, has the seventh largest natural harbor in the world, and lies on a wide plain with the sea to the south and the St Andrew Mountain as its backdrop to the north. It was founded in 1692 after an earthquake devastated the capital Port Royal.

New Kingston

The survivors moved to what is now Kingston and were able to plan a new city from scratch. It was laid out in a grid pattern, which remains today and makes it very easy to get around, especially in the downtown area. It became the capital in 1872, and considerable rebuilding was needed after an earthquake and fire on 14 January 1907 that killed almost 1,500 people.

It is now a modern, bustling, sprawling city that never seems to sleep. It is the seat of Government, has an international airport, busy port and modern cruise ship facilities, as well as a wealth of tourist facilities from accommodation to restaurants and gift shops to galleries.

The town was built on the waterfront but has gradually spread inland over the Liguanea Plains, with new business and shopping districts. **New Kingston** has emerged as the commercial heart of the capital and with its skyscrapers, is like a mini-Manhattan in New York. A major renewal scheme is underway to revitalize the former downtown area. The downtown area also houses many banking, commercial and government institutions.

Residential Kingston is a charming mix of old and new, with wonderful traditional gingerbread homes with their elaborate balconies and fretwork, classic eighteenth-century Georgian mansions, and modern houses and apartment blocks. It has to be added, however, that while Kingston has many fine old buildings and some hugely expensive new ones, it also has appalling slums, especially in western Kingston. While the downtown area, close to the waterfront, is the place to explore, the heart of Kingston is now in New Kingston, a triangular area to the north, largely bordered by Half Way Tree Road, Old Hope Road and Hope Road.

EXPLORING KINGSTON ON FOOT

Start your walking tour by the cruise ship piers in front of Ocean Boulevard, although cruise ships no longer call at Kingston. The area just inshore, between Princess Street and Duke Street which both run inland parallel with each other, contain a number of interesting buildings. The Oceana often hosts live conferences, and the main post office is on Temple Lane.

Kingston Mall runs between Princess Street and King Street parallel with and one block in from Ocean Boulevard. **The National Art Gallery** ☎: 922-1561, is between Orange Street and King Street. Open from 10am to 5pm daily, it is in the Roy West Building with exhibits about Jamaica's art history and featuring many of the island's most talented artists. There is a fantastic bronze statue of Bob Marley on the ground floor, and upstairs there are works by Intuitive artists John Dunkley, David Miller and Sidney McLaren, sculptress Edna Manley and modern pieces by Tina Matkovic, Colin Garland and Mallico Reynolds, known as Kapo, and regarded as one of Jamaica's modern artistic geniuses. The annual exhibition, featuring the

island's best artists, is held from December to January.

Off Ocean Boulevard between Church Street and Duke Street is the **Jamaica Conference Center** with its ultra-modern convention hall. It is open on Thursday only between 11am and 2pm Tel: 922-9160. It has on-site restaurants, gardens, offices and in-bond and souvenir shops that are open daily.

On the other side of Duke Street are the headquarters of the Bank of Jamaica. **The Coin and Notes Museum** is in the Bank of Jamaica building and exhibits the history of Jamaican tokens, coins and paper money. It is open 8.30am to 2pm, Monday to Friday ☎: 992-0750.

Head inland up Duke Street, turn right into Tower Street and continue just past the junction with East Street. On your right is the **Institute of Jamaica** ☎: 922-0620. The Institute is noted for its collection of historic documents about the Caribbean, and the National Library next door has the largest collection of books, articles and prints in the West Indies. The Institute also houses the **Natural History Museum**, formerly the Science Museum. It is the oldest museum in Jamaica and exhibits the preserved animals and plants found on the island. The Herbarium (where dried plants are stored) contains over 125,000 specimens and is the best in the Caribbean. It is open from 8.30am to 5pm, Monday to Thursday.

Keep right to Georges Lane, turn left and proceed across East Queen Street with the police headquarters on your right, and then turn left into Sutton Street, then right into Duke Lane which has many fine old buildings, including the St Andrew Scots Kirk Church Tel: 922-1818.

Headquarters House

Headquarters House is south of the junction with Beeston Street, and one of the most interesting and historic buildings in Kingston. It was originally built as part of a bizarre bet in the middle of the eighteenth century. A group of wealthy merchants decided to see who could build the most elegant mansion. Thomas Hibbert won the bet and the house was originally named Hibbert House after him. In 1814 it became the official res-idence of the island's military commander, and it is the only one of the four that survives today. It has an observation post on the roof, where Hibbert used to watch for ships approaching the water front. In 1972 it became the offices of the Colonial Secretary and was also used as a meeting place by the first legislature. It is open from 9am to 5pm, Monday to Saturday. The legislature moved into Gordon House across the junction, in 1960 and the Jamaica National Trust Commission moved in 1983.

Kings House, the gleaming white Governor General's official residence is set in 200 landscaped acres (80 hectares) at Vale Royal on Montrose Road which lies between Hope Road and Old Hope Road, and the gardens are open to the public daily. The Prime Minister's office is in Jamaica House, built in the 1960s and originally the official residence. Continue over the junction with Charles Street to visit

Kingston Synagogue on the right. The United Congregation of Israelites is the island's only synagogue.

William Grant Park

Retrace your steps to Charles Street, turn right and then left into Love Street and head for **William Grant Park**. Just before the Park which is in the heart of downtown Kingston is the 1,000-seat **Ward Theatre**. There has been theater, both indoor and open air, of one kind or another on this site for more than 200 years. The present theater, rebuilt after the 1907 earthquake, is now most famous for its unique Jamaican pantomime season which opens each year on 26 December, although there are musical and theatrical events throughout the year ☎: 922-0453.

The park is more often referred to as the Parade, so called because it used to house military barracks before these were moved to Up Park Camp in the middle of the eighteenth century. Today, the Parade and adjacent streets, especially to the east, bustle with activity during the day. There is the Coronation produce market with its hagglers (street vendors), and it is not un-usual to see street musicians or religious temperance groups. The Parade also boasts a bandstand, fountains and open-air theater. It is also the terminal for many of the town's buses.

Cross over the park to Kingston Parish Church on South Parade. The church was rebuilt in 1909, two years after being destroyed in the earthquake.

Buses for the airport leave from across the junction of North Parade and West Queen Street. If you continue westwards along South Parade

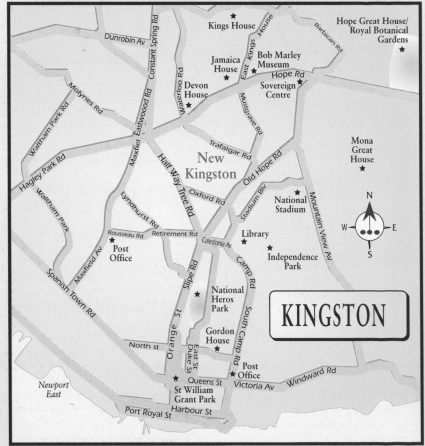

Kings House

Hope Great House/
Royal Botanical
Gardens

Dunrobin Av

Constant Spring Rd

East Kings House

Barbican Rd

Jamaica
House

Bob Marley
Museum

Waterloo Rd

Devon
House

Hope Rd

Sovereign
Centre

Molynes Rd

Waltham Park Rd

Maxfiel Eastwoood Rd

Mustgrave Rd

Trafalgar Rd

Mona
Great
House

Hagley Park Rd

New
Kingston

Half Way Tree Rd

Oxford Rd

Old Hope Rd

Waltham Park

Lyndhurst Rd

Mountain View Av

N

Rousseau Rd

Retirement Rd

Caledonia Av

Stadium Blv

National
Stadium

W   E

Maxfield Av

Post
Office

Library

S

Spanish Town Rd

Slipe Rd

Camp Rd

Independence
Park

North st

Orange St

National
Heros
Park

South Camp Rd

Gordon
House

East St

Duke St

Post
Office

Newport
East

Queens St

Victoria Av

Windward Rd

Port Royal St

St William
Grant Park

Harbour St

KINGSTON

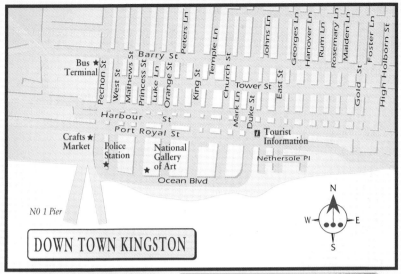

Opposite page left:
Old Kingston Harbour

Opposite page right:
Devon House

Left: Bob Marley Museum, Kingston

and then Beckford Street, you reach its junction with Pechon Street where many of the buses leave for areas outside Kingston, and the railway station is off Barry Street that runs off Pechon Street.

Shopping Area

From the parish church head south on King Street, the main shopping street, with as many stalls and vendors on the street as there are in the shops. The Post office is just beyond the junction with Barry Street. Continue south, and then turn right into Harbour Street, and left into Pechon Street to visit the **Victoria Crafts Market** on the waterfront that caters for the tourists hunting souvenirs. It offers woodcarving, woven goods, linen and silk batiks and other island crafts.

Take Ocean Boulevard back down towards the harbor to complete the tour.

PORT ROYAL AND THE PALISADOES

A drive to **Port Royal** is also a must. The island stands at the end of the **Palisadoes**, a promontory that nearly encircles the waterfront. Port Royal has a long and interesting history and has had many names, both official and unofficial. It was originally called Cayo de Carena, because Spanish vessels would be hauled on shore and then laid on their sides so the hulls could be careened – repaired and cleared of barnacles. The English named it the Point, and realizing its strategic importance built Fort Cromwell, later renamed

Fort Charles. It was the first of six forts to be built manned by a garrison of more than 2,500 men. A town developed to service the needs of the garrison, its soldiers and the pirates who also used it as a base, and at one time there were said to have been one inn or rum shop for every ten residents, and this gave rise to some of its nicknames, including the Babylon of the West, City of Gold and Sin City. One writer described it as: 'the richest, wickedest city in Christendom'.

Memorable Past

A blind eye was turned on the activities of the pirates as they attacked Spanish shipping, which suited the British authorities, and then they spent their ill-gotten gains in Port Royal adding to its prosperity. At one stage there were 2,000 buildings crammed into the town, many built on stilts over the water. One of Port Royal's most famous sons was Henry Morgan. Born in Wales, he ran away to sea and became an adventurer sailing out of Port Royal. His many exploits included the sacking of Panama in 1671 even though Britain and Spain had by then signed a peace deal. He was summoned to London to explain himself but instead of being punished, he was knighted and sent back to Jamaica as Lieutenant Governor. A century later, Admiral Horatio Nelson was also stationed on Port Royal, first as a newly appointed naval lieutenant and then as the captain of a frigate.

On 7 June 1692, Port Royal was struck by a massive earthquake and tidal wave. More than 2,000 people died and most of the buildings were destroyed with many literally falling into the sea or the huge crevices that opened up. The tidal wave was so powerful that it lifted one vessel in the harbor and dropped it on the roofs of the ruined buildings. The causeway that connected Port Royal to the Palisadoes was also swept away. Legend has it that the bell in the church tower which fell into the sea, can still sometimes be heard tolling from beneath the waves.

Although work started on rebuilding Port Royal almost immediately, the town was gutted by fire in 1703, and many residents decided it was time to relocate. The Royal Navy stayed on and Port Royal was their main Caribbean base until 1905. Because of the naval presence, there were also traders but these gradually moved to Kingston as the mainland settlement grew. Port Royal was hit by Hurricane Gilbert in 1988 but escaped remarkably unscathed, and there are many buildings and museums to explore. After your explorations you can enjoy a tasty snack and then perhaps visit one of many nearby cays for a swim or snorkel.

Fort Charles is at the western tip of The Palisadoes and is very well preserved with its rows of semi-circular gun ports in the fading red brickwork. The young lieutenant Nelson was stationed here, and a plaque in his memory reads: 'You who tread in his footprints, remember his glory'.

Fort Charles Maritime Museum exhibits displays of man's relationship to the sea from the times of the Arawaks, and traces the

Jamaican Jonah

St Peter's Church was built in 1725 replacing Christ Church that was engulfed by the sea during the 1692 earthquake. In the church there is a plaque to Louis Galdy, Jamaica's equivalent of Jonah who was swallowed by the whale. During the 1692 earthquake Galdy fell into a huge crevice and disappeared. Later the storm seas raced into the crevice and he was miraculously thrown back onto land unscathed. He is buried in the churchyard. It is claimed, although not proven, that the ceremonial silver communion vessels once belonged to Henry Morgan. The church also has a number of interesting plaques and tombstones.

development of Jamaican maritime history. There is a scale model of the fort and models of ships of past eras. It is located in the old British naval headquarters and is open from 10am to 4pm, daily.

The National Museum of Historical Archaeology is located in what used to be the naval hospital that spent a lot of its time fighting epidemics of yellow fever. The museum displays the history of the Jamaican people and techniques of excavation being used in the study of Port Royal's history based on marine and land deposits. It is open from 10am to 5pm, Monday to Saturday.

Giddy House close to the fort, is a former artillery store, and gets its name because of its strange tilt, the result of having been moved by the 1907 earthquake. Port Royal Marine Laboratory of the University of the West Indies is based in Port Royal. Founded in 1955, the laboratory began as a small room in the Old Naval Dockyard but later moved to a one-acre site, 'Crab Hall' beside the Navy Hospital. The Port Royal Laboratory has been important in undergraduate teaching of marine biology and marine ecology and in recent years has undertaken

courses in aquaculture, fisheries and coastal management. For additional information on Marine Sciences, contact the Centre for Marine Science, University of the West Indies, P.O. Box 32, Kingston, Jamaica, W. l. ☎: 927-1660

As you head back along the promontory, you can spot the remains of other fortifications and be on the look out for wildlife. The whole area is protected and home to a large number of birds, animals and reptiles.

OTHER THINGS TO SEE AND DO IN AND AROUND KINGSTON.

The African Museum is in the gleaming white Devon House complex on the corner of Hope Road and Waterloo Road. It was established in 1971. It contains artifacts relating to Jamaica's African Heritage.

Devon House, a national monument, is an elegant white three story Georgian-style Great House built in 1881 by George Stiebel, the Caribbean's first black millionaire. It has been beautifully restored by the National Trust. It contains one of the world's finest collections

The following symbols are used: $ inexpensive, $$ moderate, $$$ expensive.

Akbar $$
Indian, Holborn Road, ☎: 926-3480

Alexander's $$
International and Caribbean, Courtleigh Hotel, ☎: 929-9000

Bamboo Village $$
Chinese, Village Plaza, ☎: 926-8863

Barons $$-$$$
Continental, Braemar Avenue, ☎: 927-7114

Blue Derby $$
Steaks, seafood and Island fare, Devon House, ☎: 968-5488

Blue Mountain Inn $$
International, ☎: 927-2606

Brasserie $$
Caribbean bistro, Jamaica Pegasus, ☎: 926-3690

Bullseye $$
Steakhouse, Knutsford Blvd, ☎: 960-8724

Calcutta $$
Indian, Holburn Road, ☎: 960-0211

Country Kitchen $$
Jamaica, Jamaica Pegasus, ☎: 926-3690

Devonshire Grill $-$$
Jamaican-Continental, Devon House, ☎: 929-7046

Dragon Court $$
Chinese, Dragon Centre, ☎: 920-8506

The Eatery $
Jamaican fast food, The Mirage Disco, ☎: 978-8557

Eden $-$$
Ethiopian-Vegetarian, Central Plaza, ☎: 926-3051

El Dorado $$
Jamaican-International Terra Nova Hotel, ☎: 926-2211

Fish Pot Jamaican
Constant Spring Road, ☎: 925-7188

Food For Life $-$$
Vegetarian-Ethiopian, Dumfries Road, ☎: 926-5609

Gordon's Restaurant $$
Far East, Trafalgar Road, ☎: 929-7046

Grog Shoppe $$
English pub fare, Devon House, ☎:929-7027

Guilt Trip $-$$
Barbican Road, Kingston, ☎: 977-5130

Heathers $$
Jamaican-Middle Eastern, Haining Road, ☎: 926-2826

Hotel Four Seasons $$
Jamaican-Continental, Hotel Four Seasons, ☎: 926-8805

Hot Pot $-$$
Jamaican, Altamont Terrace, ☎: 929-3906

Indies $-$$
English, Jamaican, Holburn Road, ☎: 926-2952

Isabella's $$-$$$
Fine dining and magnificent views, Crowne Plaza Hotel, ☎: 925-7676

Ivor's $$-$$$
Gourmet, Jacks Hill, ☎: 927-1460

Jade Garden $$
Chinese, Hope Road, ☎: 978-3476

Lychee Gardens $$
Chinese, Dominica Drive,
☎: 929-8619

Mandarin Restaurant $$
Cantonese, Northside Drive,
☎: 927-0237

Mayfair $$-$$$
Continental, Mayfair Hotel,
☎: 926-1610

**Mee Mee
Restaurant Chinese**
Northside Drive, ☎: 927-9361

Minnie's $-$$
Vegetarian, Old Hope Road,
☎: 927-9207

New China Town $$
Chinese, Constant Spring Road,

**Norma's on the
Terrace $$**
Jamaican, Devon House,
☎: 968-5488

Pagoda $$
Chinese, Belmont Road, ☎: 926-2561

The Palm $$
Seafood and local, Christar Villas,
☎: 978-8066

Palm Court $$
Italian, Hilton Kingston Hotel,
☎: 926-5430

Peppers $-$$
Jamaican, Upper Waterloo Road,
☎: 925-2219

Port Royal $$-$$$
International-Seafood,
Pegasus Hotel, ☎: 926-3690

Queen of Sheba $-$$
Ethiopian, Hope Road, ☎: 978-0510

Raphael's $$
Italian, Hill Crest Avenue,
☎: 978-1279

Red Bones $$
Southern cuisine, live jazz and
blues, Braemar Avenue, ☎: 978-8262

Sea Witch $$
Seafood, Knutsford Boulevard,
☎: 929-4386

The Setting $$
International, Phoenix Avenue,
☎: 926-7830

Sir Henry's $$$
Gourmet Seafood-Jamaican-
Continental, Morgan Harbour Hotel,
☎: 924-8464

Strawberry Hill, $$-$$$
Jamaican/Continental, Irish Town,
Blue Mountains, ☎: 944-8400

Terra Nova $$-$$$
Jamaican-Continental, Terra Nova
Hotel, ☎: 929-4933

Terrace Cafe $$-$$$
Jamaican-Continental, Wyndham
Kingston Hotel, ☎: 926-5430

Jamaica fast food outlets: Brick
Oven, Devon House; Chelsea Jerk
Centre, Chelsea Avenue; Fee Fee,
South Avenue; Fish Place, Constant
Spring Road; Peppers, Upper
Waterloo Road; Roti Bazaar, Sover-
eign Centre; and Tastee , Knutsford
Boulevard,

of antique mahogany furniture. A large shaded verandah runs round the ground floor, and there are balconies on the first floor with great views over the gardens and surrounding countryside. In the landscaped grounds with towering palms and lush vegetation, are a Port Royal-style grog shop, Norma's on the Terrace restaurant specializing in Jamaican cuisine, craft shop, souvenir shop, and a ice cream shop where you can try delicious tropical fruit tasting ices. It is open from 10am to 5pm, Tuesday to Saturday ☎: 929-7029.

The Bob Marley Museum is further along at 56 Hope Road on the corner with Marley Road. It opened in 1986 and was formerly Bob Marley's residence and the site of the Tuff Gong recording studio. It contains an incredible mural 'The Journey of Bob Marley Superstar', painted by Everald Brown, and has a collection of Marley memorabilia depicting the life and career of the late reggae superstar. No photography is allowed. It is open 9.30am to 5pm, Monday, Tuesday, Thursday and Friday, and 12.30pm to 6pm on Wednesday, Saturday and public holidays ☎: 927-9152

Caymanas Park offers horse racing every Wednesday, Saturday, and on public holidays. 12.30p.m. to 6.00p.m. The course is in Waterford to the west of Kingston and is best reached by taking the Causeway from Marcus Garvey Drive in the city center.

The Folk Musical Instrument Exhibition opened as a teaching aid to Jamaica School of Music in 1981, and contains unusual musical instruments collected between 1966 and 1981. **The Geology Museum** exhibits rocks and minerals of Jamaica and collections from other countries, many of them rare.

The **Hope Botanical Gardens** are on Old Hope Road past Jamaica College and next to the College of Arts, Science and Technology. Founded in 1881, it is the largest botanical gardens in the West Indies, covering 200 acres (80 hectares). The huge lawns are surrounded by towering royal palms. It is open daily from 8.30am to 6.30pm ☎: 927-1257.

The **Jamaica Defense Force Museum** (Military Museum) is in Up Park Camp, off South Camp Road. There are fascinating plans of the many forts built around Kingston in the eighteenth century, as well as information, weapons, medals and uniforms of the West Indies Regiment and the Jamaica Infantry Militia that existed from 1662 to 1906. It is open from 10am to 5pm, Monday to Friday, and visits are by appointment.

Liguanea is north of New Kingston and site of the Sovereign Centre, the capital's newest shopping complex, with cinemas, banks and a food hall. **Lime Cay** is a glorious sunspot off Kingston's shore. South of The Palisadoes the uninhabited island can be reached by boat and it is great for swimming and snorkeling. It is open all day, daily.

The National Arena and National Stadium are side by side off State Road that runs off Mountain View Avenue on the eastern side of town. The arena is used for a wide range of activities from trade exhibitions to the Caribbean's largest flower show, the National Festival Song Competition and the Festival King and Queen Costume Show ☎: 929-4970. Close by the arena is another fine bronze of Marley.

Heroes Park

The National Heroes Park, reached by East Street from downtown, has many statues and monuments dedicated to the island's heroes, as well as a number of tombs. There are monuments to Paul Bogle and George Gordon, heroes of the Morant Bay rebellion, and the tombs of Marcus Garvey, Norman Manley and Alexander Bustamante.

Port Henderson lies to the south west of the capital connected to it by a causeway that runs from Kingston waterfront across Hunts Bay to Portmore. When Spanish Town was the island capital, Port Henderson was the main harbor and protected by two forts – Fort Clarence and Fort Augusta, and it became a fashionable nineteenth-century spa resort. The town was badly damaged by the 1951 hurricane and is now a small coastal community opposite Port Royal.

It is worth visiting as a number of its older buildings have been restored or their ruins uncovered by the National Trust. These include the ruins of **Green Castle Great House** and **Bullock's Lodge** and the **Longhouse**, which was an inn until the end of the nineteenth century. **Fort Clarence** stood at the end of an arid promontory to the south of Port Henderson and guards the harbor approaches. Today you can enjoy a swim off Fort Clarence Beach or Hellshire Beach to the south. The Arawaks were early settlers in this area and there are petroglyphs in Two Sisters Cave at Hellshire Beach.

It is a small white sand beach with nearby steps that lead down to the 200,000 year-old cave below sea level.

The area also has interesting vegetation and wildlife adapted to the very dry conditions, including some iguana. **The Rockfort Mineral Baths** are in a natural mineral spa on the coast on Windward Road (A4) that runs east out of Kingston ☎: 938-5055.

Sabina Park on South Camp Road is where you go if you want to experience a West Indian cricket match.

The University of the West Indies is off Old Hope Road on the eastern outskirts of town. Turn off on to Mona Road, past the Mona Reservoir to reach the university campus, originally part of the Mona Sugar Estate. You can stroll around the campus where there are old aqueducts, machinery and other reminders of its agricultural past alongside modern murals. The chapel close to the entrance used to be a sugar warehouse on the Gales Valley Estate in Trelawny. It was taken down brick by brick and re-built on its present site. Under the roof you can make out the name of the original owner and the date when it was first built.

The university is open from 9am to 5pm, Monday to Saturday. The Zoology Museum, operated by the University of the West Indies houses exhibits similar to those at the Natural History Museum, but contains many more animals. The marine and entomology collections are considered the best in the West Indies. The **University's Creative Arts Centre** has a varied program of student productions. The University Carnival is held during February ☎: 927-1660.

Kingston Galleries

Amalcraft
Red Hills Road, ☎: 920-9168

Antiquarian and Trading Co.
30 Hope Road, ☎: 926-8778

The Art Gallery
10 Gareli Avenue, ☎: 926-5097

The Artisan
14 Dominica Drive, ☎: 978-8514

Babylon Jamaica
10 A. W. King's House Road,
☎: 926-0416

Bolivar Books/Gallery
1D Grove Road, ☎: 926-8799

Chelsea Galleries
12 Chelsea Avenue, ☎: 929-0045

Contemporary Art Centre
1 Liguanea Avenue, ☎: 927-9958

Essel Gallery
Old Hope Road,
☎: 977-2067

Four Corners Gallery
7 West Arcadia Avenue, ☎: 929-2846

Frame Art
1 Belmont Road,
☎: 926-5014

Frame Centre Gallery
10 Tangerine Place, ☎: 926-4644

Gallery Makonde
Wyndham Kingston Hotel,
☎: 977-4409

Gallery Pegasus
Jamaica Pegasus, ☎: 926-3690

The Garden Gallery
1 Mannings Hill Road, ☎: 925-2272

Grosvenor Galleries
Grosvenor Terrace, ☎: 924-6684

Hi Qo
Spanish Court, ☎: 926-4183

Institute of Jamaica
12 East Street, ☎: 922-0620

Medallion Galleries
Hope Road, ☎:

Mutual Life Gallery
2 Oxford Road, ☎: 929-4302

National Gallery of Art
12 Ocean Boulevard, ☎: 922-1561

Olympla International Art Centre
202 Old Hope Road
☎: 927-1608

The Palette
21 Haining Road, ☎: 929-8203

Patoo
Constant Spring Road
☎: 924-1552

Statements Photoart Gallery
14 Carvalho Drive, ☎: 929-2072

Serigraphics Jamaica
70 Hanover Street, ☎: 922-2072

Things Jamaican
Devon House, 26 Hope Road,
☎: 929-6602

Upstairs Downstairs
108 Harbour Street, ☎: 922-8260

The Wanderer
Queensway, ☎: 926-6071

Above: Reach Falls
Right: Manchioneal
Below: Long Bay Vendors Market

THE EASTERN TOUR

Take the A4 that runs eastwards along the south coast from Kingston through Rockfort to Fort Nugent. The road continues past Seven Mile and Palm Beach, Copacabana and Bull Bay. From Bull Bay you can detour inland to Newstead and then visit the falls on the Cane River, and at Eleven Mile, you can make another small detour inland to visit the falls near Newstead.

The coast road continues to Grants Pen and Albion where you can detour inland to Ellington on the Yallahs River. There are good views here of the massive escarpment known as **Judgement Cliff**, a lasting reminder of the 1692 earthquake. The cliff is said to have got its name because during the upheaval that created it, a landslide destroyed the plantation of a cruel owner – a fitting judgment.

Drive past Poor Man's Corner to the lovely beaches at **Flemarie** and **Bailey's** near **Yallahs**. West of Yallahs the road runs past the **Salt Ponds** which run for more than 5 miles (8km) past Pomfret to Green Wall. Seawater evaporates in the shallow ponds and the Indians and early settlers collected the salt that was left.

1865 Uprising

Morant Bay is the chief town of St Thomas Parish, although it is little more than a village. Its main claim to fame is as the site of the Paul Bogle-led uprising in 1865 when the Baptist minister led about 400 of his followers to Morant Bay Court House on 11 October to hand over a list of grievances. The authorities, alerted of this, called out the local volunteer militia. In the running battles that followed, the Court House was burned down and many townspeople lost their lives. Martial law was declared and the troops rushed in, burnt down more than 1,000 homes and executed after summary trial more than 400 men and women.

Governor Eyre also used the rebellion as an excuse to rid himself of George Gordon, a member of the legislature and an outspoken champion of the poor. Gordon was brought in chains from Kingston to Morant Bay and falsely accused by witnesses of being the rebellion ringleader. He was found guilty and publicly hanged with Paul Bogle in front of the burned-out courthouse. Shortly afterwards the Governor was recalled to London in disgrace and Jamaica from then on was administered as a Crown Colony. The courthouse was rebuilt and a statue of Bogle, sculpted by Edna Manley, stands in front of it. Excavations in the mid-1970s inside Morant Bay Fort discovered the skeletons of 79 people whose bodies had been hidden in rubbish dumps.

The stone signal tower is a listed national monument.

There are fine beaches at **Lyssons** and **Retreat**, and then the road runs inland round the large bay on which **Port Morant** and **Bowden** stand. Both were once prosperous ports loading ships with bananas and sugar cane, and the flat area of land east of Bowden down to the sea is known as Holland. It was once owned by Simon Taylor, the richest sugar cane plantation owner on Jamaica, and perhaps the wealthiest man in the West Indies. Just east of Golden Grove is **Stokes Hall**, one of the island's oldest plantations.

Healing Waters

At Hordley you can take the road for an interesting detour to Bath six miles (10km) due west inland. The town was named because of its hot springs and the official name is The Bath of St Thomas the Apostle. Legend has it that the first spring, deep in the forest, was discovered by a runaway slave at the end of the seventeenth century. He bathed his ulcerated legs in the warm water and gradually the ulcers healed. It is said that he then rushed back to tell his owner about the curative waters. It is not known what the owner thought of this story or what happened to the slave!

In the eighteenth century the town that developed became a fashionable spa resort, but today little remains other than the **Bath Fountain Hotel** ☎: 982-2132, housing the baths and the botanical gardens. There are both hot and cold water springs feeding the baths, and the high sulfur content can be smelt in the air. The waters are said to be particularly beneficial for people with skin complaints or rheumatic ailments. The botanical gardens are the second oldest in the Western Hemisphere, and although past their heyday, they contain many fascinating trees and plants. Many of the new species introduced to the island were planted here first, and many of their offspring survive, including plants grown from the first breadfruit tree brought by Captain Bligh. From Bath there is a path over the mountains to Four Feet at the end of the road that runs north into Port Antonio.

You can drive down to the southeast tip of the island at **Morant Point Lighthouse**. This is a very marshy area with reefs offshore. The bay to the southwest must have been a dangerous place for ships, thus its name of Folly Bay.

The route then continues along the eastern coastline through Hectors River and Manchioneal where you should detour to visit the delightful **Reach Falls**, reached by taking the inland road off the A4 just over one mile (1.6km). The largest of the falls is about 40ft (12m) high, and you can swim in the pools or picnic nearby.

Long Bay has a fabulous beach, and **Boston Bay** has a popular bathing beach beneath towering cliffs, and the waves are high enough for surfing. The famous Jamaican dish 'Jerk Pork', originated in this area, and was passed down from the Maroons. There is a nice beach at **Fairy Hill** with changing rooms and showers.

The Blue Lagoon, also known as Blue Hole, is a mineral-rich lagoon, which according to legend is bottomless. Take the side road that runs downhill from the A4 to the water's edge. The lagoon is, in fact, about 210ft (64m) deep, but the waters are remarkably clear because of a mix of salt and freshwater. The salt water comes from the Caribbean and blends with freshwater from several underground streams that run into the lagoon. The steeply sloping walls of the lagoon are also rich in minerals, including the semi-precious lapis lazuli. The stretch of coastline from the Blue Lagoon to Port Antonio has some of the island's most exclusive resorts.

San San Beach is one of the prettiest beaches along this stretch of coast and is rarely busy other than at weekends. **Monkey Island** lies just off-shore, and although the little island is still covered in trees and lush vegetation, there are no monkeys – if indeed, there ever were any.

Just inland are the **Caves of Nonsuch** and the **Gardens of Athenry**. The caves are set in the 185-acre (74 hectare) of tropical rain forest 1,000ft (305m) above sea level in the Seven Hills Of Athenry Garden Plantation. You can see fossilized sea sponges, volcanic rock, clamshells and a frozen waterfall. There are winding paths through the caves that are lit to show the stalactites and stalagmites, and other limestone formations. There are daily 30-minute guided tours. The caves and gardens are open from 9am to 5pm daily ☎: 993-3740.

New Mall, Port Antonio

Above: Port Antonio   Below: Belle View looking towards Port Antonio bay

Trident Castle

Trident Castle

On the headland, there is an imposing castle. As you drive along the winding coast road it suddenly appears in front of you, and it took one bus driver so much by surprise that he drove straight off the road into the sea. There are lots of myths about the castle, but it was actually built by prominent architect Earl Levy who owns the adjoining Trident Villas and Hotel, and it is known as Trident Castle. The Levy family is one of the oldest on the island and the castle is not currently open to the public although this may change as part of the hotel's expansion plans. Even if you are not planning to stay overnight, it is worth visiting the Trident Villas and Hotel that boasts lovely gardens, a very good restaurant and some very friendly peacocks and guinea fowl. It is also a charming place to stop for afternoon tea.

Trident Castle should not be confused with the Jamaica Palace that is a little further along on the opposite side of the road. Built by a German lady who expanded it into a magnificent house, it is now the centerpiece of the Jamaica Palace hotel.

Port Antonio is on the island's northeast coast and is a charming blend of old and new. It was Jamaica's first tourist resort and although still popular as a resort with cruise ship facilities, it is in need of a face-lift, and a campaign has been mounted locally to get Government funds for this. It has, however, managed to retain much of its quiet fishing village charm. The location could not be more perfect with sheltered harbor, beautiful scenery and landscapes inland, and long stretches of stunning white sandy beaches.

The scenery is obviously good for inspiration, as Port Antonio is a favorite area for writers and artists, and Robin Moore is said to have written the French Connection while sitting under a mango tree in his yard. It has also long been popular with the rich and famous, and was a playground of Royalty and movie stars like Errol Flynn, Ginger Rogers and Bette Davis. It also claims to have been used as a setting for more films than anywhere else in the Caribbean.

The town was named Puerto Anton by the first Spanish, and although the English settlers renamed it Titchfield, the original name has survived. Titchfield was also the name of the estate of Lord Portland, a former Governor, after whom the parish is named. Land grants were offered to Europeans to boost settlement and the town was fortified to protect both the harbor and the residents who were heavily outnumbered by slaves in the surrounding plantations, and there were a number of uprisings.

The main part of Port Antonio is shaped like a horseshoe around the large East Harbour. On the eastern tip of the horseshoe is Folly Point Lighthouse, and Fort George was built on the shorter western tip known as Titchfield Peninsula. Navy Island stands off Titchfield Peninsula and although known as Lynch Island, after an early Governor, was renamed because it was fortified and used by the navy as a hospital and land base in the 1720s. Over the years the town has expanded westwards and now includes West Harbour, which is why Port Antonio is sometimes referred to as the Twin Harbours. The Twin Harbours were described by American poet Ella Willa Wilcox, as the 'most exquisite port on earth', and are great places to fish for marlin, tarpon and red snapper.

Today Port Antonio is popular with those seeking a more peaceful, relaxing holiday although there is still plenty to see and do for those who want to get around. There are lots of restaurants and bars, and shopping along Harbour Street and City Centre Plaza. The offshore waters offer great game fishing and there are a number of fishing tournaments from the Marina.

The tourist office is in the **City Centre Plaza** (☎: 993-3051). A good way to get your bearings is to walk up Bonnie View, the road that runs up Richmond Hill to the vantage point near the summit which has magnificent views of the town and surrounding areas. It is a great place to watch the sunset. There are historical tours of the town from the sea, and details are available from the tourist office, but the town is easy and fun to explore on foot.

Start by exploring **Titchfield Peninsula**. In 1947 Errol Flynn arrived in town and immediately fell in love with it. Ironically, in one of his swashbuckling films, he had played adventurer Henry Morgan, who became Lieutenant Governor of Jamaica. Flynn bought the Titchfield Hotel, which he renamed Jamaica Reef, and also purchased Navy Island.

The town became very fashionable in the 1950s and was the haunt of the rich and famous. Many of the buildings in the area, including the hotel, were destroyed by fire. Titchfield School was built on the site of the hotel, and nearby is the

Banana Trade

The area's prosperity really dates from the 1870s and the start of the banana trade between Jamaica and Britain and the United States. Bananas had been imported from Hispaniola by the Spanish but they were largely used for animal feed. They were not exported because there was thought to be no demand for them, and even if there were, the bananas would be rotten before they could be sold.

It was not until 1871 that Captain Lorenzo Dow Baker realized that bananas could be shipped if they were picked very green and allowed to ripen on board. His first shipment to Boston sold for $2,000. He helped found the Boston Fruit Company and the banana trade was born. Estates flourished and many large houses were built. The DeMontevin Lodge Guest House ☎: 993-2604, was one of those built during the banana boom, and it has the typical ornate fretwork on balconies and under the eaves, that characterizes the Caribbean gingerbread style.

shell of the hotel staff quarters and two swimming pools that used to belong to the hotel. The site has now been taken over by the Jamaican Defence Force and is used as a training camp. You can visit the eighteenth-century Christ Church that is still in use.

Fort George with its 10ft (3m) thick walls, is mostly in ruins but the Titchfield School, founded in 1785, is housed in the former barracks. Other sights on the peninsula include De Montevin Lodge, an historic landmark, and the former home of an admiral. At the neck of the peninsula around the junction of Harbour Street and West Street are the Court House, Capitol Cinema and Market.

There is a pleasant walk along the Harbour Street, past the Anglican Christ Church, built in the early 1840s, and Allan Avenue that follows the harbor's edge to the eastern arm of the horseshoe. There is a road off the A4 that leads through the Folly Estate where you can visit Mitchell's Folly and the Folly Point Lighthouse.

Navy Island

You can take the ferry for the seven-minute boat ride across to Navy Island and spend as long as you like as the boats operate 24 hours a day. Conducted tours of the island can be arranged. After Errol Flynn bought it, he imported exotic birds and planted hundreds of palms and other tropical plants. Today, there are African-style cottages and villas, the Admiralty Club with its fabulous marina, three beaches and watersports. The Club's bar has a room of Errol Flynn memorabilia. The island is still a great place for birding with many sea birds, egrets, white owls and peregrine falcons. When Errol Flynn was not sailing in the Caribbean, he used to anchor his yacht *Zacca*, off the seven-acre (2.8 hectare) island.

Navy Island

EATING OUT

• IN AND AROUND PORT ANTONIO •

Eating out in and around Port Antonio
The following symbols are used: $ inexpensive, $$ moderate, $$$ expensive.

Admiralty Club $$-$$$
Jamaican-Continental ☎: 993-2667

Bamboo Grill Room $-$
Jamaican-International, Dragon Inn ☎: 993-3281

Blue lagoon $-$$
Jamaican-International, live jazz Friday ☎: 993-8491

Bonnie View $$
Excellent Jamaican, Bonnie View Plantation Hotel ☎: 993-2752

DeMontevin Lodge Jamaican
☎: 993-2604

Fern Hill Club $$
Jamaican-International, superb views, ☎: 993-7374

Grill Restaurant $$
Jamaican-Continental, Dragon Bay Villas ☎: 993-3281

Huntress Marina $$
casual waterfront dining, seafood ☎: 993-3053

Jamaican Palace Hotel $$-$$$
Gourmet, ☎: 993-2020

Pavilion $$
Nouvelle cuisine with Jamaican twists, Dragon Bay Beach Resort, ☎: 993-8514

Rafter's Rest $-$$
Jamaican-International, Rio Grande Rafting Centre ☎: 993-2778

San San Tropez $$
Italian, opposite Frenchman's Cove, ☎: 993-7213

Trident $$-$$$
Elegant Caribbean-Continental, Trident Villa and Hotel ☎: 993-2602. Afternoon tea, reservations for dinner required.

Crumbling Folly

The Folly was built in 1905 by a wealthy American, Alfred Mitchell from Connecticut He also helped design the house and it is said his wife disliked it so much, that she refused to set foot in it. He visited from time to time until his death in 1912. The Mansion was built to withstand hurricanes using concrete and reinforced steel. Legend has it that salt water was used to mix the concrete during the construction and the salt corroded the steel and the structure started to crumble in the 1930s. In fact, this is not true, but soft marl was used in the construction and the building was sited in such a way that it caught the full brunt of onshore winds and salt-borne spray, and it was this that caused the erosion. In 1938 the roof finally collapsed, and the house remained derelict.

In the late 1940s it was acquired by the Government, and for a time was leased to Mrs. Errol Flynn who planned to develop it into a resort. The project collapsed like the house, although the crumbling structure, with some interesting graffiti, impressive columns, arches and stone steps, can be seen. It is possible to swim from the nearby beach over to **Wood Island**. The red and white striped Folly Point Lighthouse stands at the end of the promontory.

A wide range of tours are organized from Port Antonio including trips into the **Blue Mountains**. There are tours of the **Blue Mountain Coffee Plantations** and even a Blue Mountain Cycle Ride on mountain bikes, led by experienced guides. Port Antonio-based Valley Hikes offer conducted walks, raft trips, waterfall and caving visits in the Rio Grande Valley.

Rafting down the **Rio Grande** is another exciting outing, and is said to have been started by Errol Flynn. Rio Grande Rafting offer 6 mile (10km) cruises on bamboo rafts for two, poled by expert raftsmen through spectacular scenery. The trip can take between two and three hours. About 150 rafters operate on the river, and they follow the route traditionally taken by the Maroons, and later used to transport bananas to the sea. The Rafters Pavilion is at Rafters Rest at the mouth of the river and was built by the Earl of Mansfield. If not on an organized tour, drive to Rafters Rest to pick up a driver who will take you to the start point, and then drive your hire car back so that it is waiting for you. Do

The Moore Town Maroons

There is an interesting detour inland from Port Antonio to Fellowship, Windsor and Seaman's Valley. Take the left fork for Moore Town and the Maroon Museum. There was a large Maroon settlement in the area around Moore Town, and because they were virtually self-ruling, their culture and traditions remained intact. Many of their traditional dances and ceremonies today can be traced directly back to their African roots, and have changed little over the centuries.

The most important of these ceremonies is the Kromanti Drum Dance, named after the infamous slave market on the west coast of Africa in what is now Ghana, and the most traditional of all the Kromanti Dances is danced by the Moore Town Maroons. The dance is used both to communicate with ancestral spirits and for healing. It is very elaborate with the 'myal' or ritual doctor, presiding as the 'fete man'. The drumming, dancing and singing often last for hours with different styles and mood changes until the participants are 'possessed' by the beat of the drums. Sacrifices, usually chicken or small pig, often mark the climax of the dance.

Maroon music still reflects the styles of the many West African tribes it came from, such as Mandinga, from Senegal and Gambia, Ibo from Nigeria, Akans of Ghana, Mongola from Angola and Kromanti from the Gold Coast, although there has been much merging over the years.

not forget your cameras. It is available from 8.30am to 4.30pm daily ☎: 993-2778.

Moore Town is the home of the Windward Maroons, and governed by an elected committee chaired by a colonel, a reminder of the days when the Maroons were organized into military bands to fight the British. The Anglican Church at the entrance to the town, is the oldest building, and Bump Grave, opposite the school, is the tomb of Nanny, an eighteenth-century Maroon leader who was known for her fighting skills.

The site of Nanny Town is across the hills to the west of Ginger House, and you can appreciate how remote it is when you consider that British troops under orders to find the camp at all costs, took six years to locate it. When they did finally attack the town, Nanny and her Maroon troops had climbed to higher ground and poured boiling water on to the soldiers who fled. It took repeated attacks before the town was finally taken and destroyed, and now it has been taken over by the forest, and although there have been some archaeological digs, nothing of great interest has yet been found.

The road ends a little further on at Cornwall Barracks, another Maroon settlement. From here you can cross the rope bridge to visit **Jupiter Falls**, beside a mineral spring. The right fork at **Seaman's Valley** runs to **Alligator Church**, **Ginger House**, **Comfort Castle** and ends just beyond Four Feet, high in the John Crow mountains. This is the wettest place in Jamaica and annual rainfalls of 459in (1166cm) have been recorded. To your right are the peaks of Macca Sucker 4380ft (1335m) and Dinner Time 3851ft (1174m) beyond. There is a path from Four Feet across the mountains south to Bath.

The route continues westwards along the north coastline to **Hope Bay** and the **Somerset Falls**. The Daniels River plunges through a gorge of natural rock in a series of cascades and pools. The Lower falls are set in tropical gardens and the Higher falls are reached by swimming or rafting into the narrow gorge. There is a restaurant and rest rooms. The admission charge includes the raft trip, and the falls are open from 10am to 5pm daily, except Christmas and Good Friday ☎: 926-2952.

Continue to Orange Bay and Buff Bay, where you can take secondary road B1 through the mountains back to Kingston. **Crystal Spring Eco-Resort** is a 156-acre (62 hectare) recreational center with picnic ground, botanical garden, orchid forest, bird sanctuary, and apiary located in Buff Bay. The park has more than 15,000 varieties of plants and one of the largest orchid collections in the Caribbean. It is open from 9am to 6pm, daily ☎:1-800-532-2271.

Continue past Windsor Castle to Annotto Bay and then just past Grays Inn turn left on the A3 for the drive south back to Kingston through Broadgate, and Devon Pen.

At **Castleton** there are **Botanic Gardens** founded in 1859, close to the Wag Water River. The gardens have reduced in size over the years and now cover about 15 acres (6 hectares) and are still worth visiting for their exotic flora much of which is identified by labels. They contain both native and exotic species and many varieties of fruit trees found on the island ☎: 927-1257.

The road then continues through Golden Spring and Stony Hill back into Kingston.

EXPLORING THE BLUE MOUNTAINS

The Blue Mountains get their name because from a distance they actually look blue when seen through the shimmering heat haze. The mountains are a delight to visit, offer stunning scenery and are a sharp contrast to the tourist areas around the coast. The mountains are wet, receiving more than 300in (762cm) of rainfall a year, but it is this that accounts for their incredible lushness even at high altitude. The Blue Mountains occupy almost a quarter of the island, virtually all the interior land east of Kingston, known as the Eastern Highlands.

The Blue Mountains

The mountains are geologically interesting because they were formed about 25 million years ago and upheaval is still continuing, at the rate of just under one inch (2.5cm) every 100 years or so. The northern slopes of the mountains are heavily forested and receive the highest rainfall, while there has been a lot of deforestation on the southern slopes both for timber and to clear the land for crops, not all of them legal!

More than 193,260 acres (77304 hectares) of the area is now part of the Blue Mountain National Park, the largest park in Jamaica. It covers parts of the Blue Mountains, Port Royal Mountains and John Crow Mountains, and contains a huge variety of plants and animals, including the giant swallow-tailed

A view of The Blue Mountains

butterfly, *papilio homerus*, with a six inch (15cm) wingspan, found nowhere else in the world, and the Jamaican hutia. Many of the island's 27 endemic birds are also found within the park's boundaries, including the Vervain hummingbird, the rare Jamaican blackbird, and the Jamaican tody.

Above: **Dr Sangster's Rum Factory, Blue Mountains**
Below: **Buff Bay**

Blue Mountain Peak, the highest point on the island at 7402ft (2257m) is in the heart of the mountains and the John Crow Mountains run down the eastern flanks, parallel with the east coast. There are many peaks above 5000ft (1524m). The Grand Ridge has five main peaks: John Crow 5750ft (1753m), St John's 6332ft (1930m), Mossman's 6703ft (2044m), High Peak 6812ft (2077m), and Blue Mountain Peak.

There are several roads into the mountains while the A3 that runs north to Annotto Bay through Castleton offers great views along and access into the western flank. The best way of reaching Blue Mountain Peak is to take Gordon Town Road which runs north out of Kingston just past the Hope Botanical Gardens and College of Arts, Science and Technology, both on Old Hope Road.

Gordon Town is a charming small hill town where you can stop off for a relaxing drink and take in the views. The road splits at the Cooperage and you should take the right fork through Industry Village and Guava Ridge to Mavis Bank. A botanical garden was planted at Guava Ridge in the 1770s but has long since disappeared, while a short detour north leads to Content Gap and World's End, where you can visit Dr. Sangster's Rum Factory (☎: 926-8888). This small distillery was started by a Scotsman and is now a popular tourist attraction.

At Mavis bank there is a trail to Blue Mountain Peak and the **Jablum Coffee Processing Plant** that can be toured for a small fee. The roads in this area are not of the best and great care needs to be taken when driving on them. The only way to explore this area is on foot, and the walking is spectacular and in places strenuous. Temperatures are much cooler than on the coast, but it can still feel hot if you are toiling up a mountain through the humid

Climbing Blue Mountain Peak

The mountains are criss-crossed by many paths and trails but it is best to undertake trips in this area with a guide. A guide will not only ensure you do not get lost, he will ensure you get the most out of the trip by pointing out plants and birds along the way, and a host of other things that visitors normally miss. Several companies offer conducted tours to the Blue Mountain Peak and many of these leave in the early hours of the morning so that you can be on the summit to celebrate sunrise. The climb takes about three hours if you are fit and four to six hours if you are not. There are also mules for those who do not have the puff to make it on their own. The path climbs from beautiful tropical rain forest with mahogany and bamboo, through damp areas with woodland and ferns, moss underfoot and on trees, and massive air plants, to elfin woodlands as you approach the summit. The mountain woodlands have an amazing variety of orchids, many of them tiny and easily missed.

forest. There are no main highways and most of the mountain roads can only be travelled by four-wheel drive vehicles.

Camping is allowed in this area and you need to carry in all the equipment and supplies you need. There are some cabins at Clydesdale on an old coffee plantation, and Hollywell, which can be rented from the Forestry Department if booked early enough, and again it is advisable to carry in everything you will need.

If you take the left hand fork at the Cooperage, the road runs to **Newcastle**, originally a coffee estate, and then in 1814 a hill station for troops garrisoned on the island. As in India, the troops would be given leave to spend time at the hill station to escape the heat of the coast. There is now a Jamaica Defence Force Camp overlooking the Mamee River that runs south to the sea, east of Kingston. The area is still an important training camp for both island and visiting forces.

It then continues past the 300 acre (120 hectare) **Hollywell Forest Park** on your left, where there are extensive trails and camping, and

Catherine's Peak on your right to a T-junction at Section. The left fork goes to Green Hill and then on over the mountains to Buff Bay on the north coast, while the right hand fork heads east to Westphalia. The road runs just to the south and nearly parallel with the Grand Ridge of the Blue Mountains.

The **Cinchona Botanic Gardens** are on the left hand side of the mountain road near Clydesdale and before Westphalia. Despite their altitude – about 5,000ft (1524m) – the gardens have a very English feel and are surrounded by estates producing the world famous aromatic coffee. The gardens are named after the tree that was grown commercially for its bark from which quinine is obtained, although it was originally a tea plantation. As the tea estate ceased production, the gardens developed. There are many exotic plants and trees planted around the Great House as well as many native species, including the Blue Mountain Yacca. You can also visit the **Silver Hill coffee estate** while Pine Grove, another working coffee farm, offers accommodation and has a good restaurant.

Exploring the Island:
West of Kingston

THE SOUTHERN COASTAL TOUR

Take the A1 west out of Kingston past Ye Olde Ferry Inn on your right to Ferry which is on the Fresh River marking the boundary between St Andrew parish in Surrey and the parish of St Catherine in Middlesex. A little further along on the right is the *White Marle Arawak Museum*, which has displays of Arawak history, relics and culture from before Columbus. It is located on the site of the largest Arawak village on the island, and the museum is in the shape of a typical Arawak house – octagonal with a conical roof.

SPANISH TOWN

Spanish Town is about 2 miles (3.2km) along the road. It was the former capital of the island and the town square is said to be one of the finest examples of Georgian architecture in the western hemisphere. The Spanish originally called it Villa de la Vega, which means town on the plain, after abandoning their first settlement at Sevilla la Nieva on the north coast in 1534. The town came under repeated attacks from pirates and the English over the next 120 years. Finally, in 1655 the English captured it and moved in. As was the custom of the day, the English soldiers were allowed to loot the town, but the citizens had fled with almost everything of value, and in their anger they burnt most of the houses down.

The town remained the capital and was rebuilt with some splendid buildings, such as the Court House, Legislature and official residence of the Governor. Spanish Town was the administrative and judicial heart of the island, but Kingston was rapidly becoming the commercial center, and in 1755, exactly 100 years after the English took over Jamaica the capital was transferred to Kingston. After three years of litigation, however, the move was ruled illegal because Kingston merchants had bribed the Governor to sign the capital-changing decree and the King had never sanctioned it. Spanish Town became the capital again, but Kingston continued to prosper and in 1872 it was made the chief city again.

Most of the historic buildings are around the Park in the center of town, although the impressive cathedral is a few blocks south on Red Church Street. The Court House stands on the south of the Park. It was rebuilt after being destroyed by fire in 1985 and is now used for meetings.

Kings House is in King Street on the western side of the Park although only the front of the original 1762 building remains. The rest of the building was destroyed by a fire in 1925 and rebuilt. The building has a special place in Jamaican history because it was from the steps that the proclamation of Emancipation was read on 1 August 1938. It was the Governor's official residence until 1872, when the capital was transferred to Kingston. It now contains the **Archaeological Museum** with artifacts excavated at the site and exhibits tracing the history of the area between 1534-1872.

The Jamaican Peoples Museum of Craft and Technology is in the former stables block. Exhibits include implements, machinery and utensils, and displays featuring the architecture and industrial culture used throughout Jamaican history. It also traces the links between the various cultures that have merged on the island from the original Amerindians. The Post Office is further along King Street.

The **Rodney Memorial** flanked by cannon, on the northern side of the park commemorates Admiral George Rodney whose victory over the combined Spanish and French fleets at the Battle of the Saints in

1782, almost certainly prevented Jamaica from falling into enemy hands. Why sculptor John Bacon should have portrayed Rodney wearing a Roman toga and carrying a scroll, is not clear. The National Archives are next to the Memorial and contain a number of fascinating documents, including a number about the Moravian Church, a missionary sect that spread through many of the Caribbean Islands educating the slaves.

The House of Assembly on the east side of the park, was completed in 1762 although it has seen many changes since, which explains the contrast between the grand colonnade ground floor and the wooden first floor.

The Oldest Cathedral

The Cathedral of St James (Jago de la Vega) is the oldest in the West Indies and is on Red Church Street a few blocks south of the Park. It is built on the site of a Spanish chapel destroyed by English troops in 1655, and was destroyed in 1712 by a hurricane. It was rebuilt in red stone in 1714 and is the island's second oldest structure after Fort Charles. It is now the Anglican Cathedral Church for the Jamaican Diocese. It has many interesting features and some beautiful marble tombs, both inside and outside in the courtyard. It is open daily. The public library is opposite.

Other sights include the busy little Market at the end of Adelaide Street that runs west from the Park. The tin-roofed market offers local produce, T-shirts and some souvenirs. **Nature's Habitat** is a fishing and recreational facility with picnic area, playing area for children and a 9-hole mini golf course.

The Baptist Church, on the corner of French and William Streets, was built in the late 1820s but badly damaged by a hurricane in 1951. At the time of Emancipation the missionary minister was the Rev. J. M. Phillippo.

Just outside Spanish Town is **Serenity Wildlife Park and Zoo** with exotic birds, petting zoo, horseback riding, picnic area and restaurant.

You can take the A1 north out of town to Bog Walk and then the secondary road east through Jackson to **Sligoville**, the former summer home of the Governor, and the first 'free village' founded after Emancipation in 1835 when the land was bought by the Rev. Phillippo and made available to former slaves who wanted to settle there.

From Spanish Town the tour continues east on the A2. You can detour north on the small road through Innswood to **Guanaboa Vale**, where there are a number of interesting tombstones in the church cemetery. The settlement was the scene of an English mutiny in 1660. Close by is **Mountain River Cave**, noted for its Arawak rock paintings.

You can return south through Springfield and Spring Village to rejoin the A2 for the drive through Tamarind to Old Harbour. To the south is Old Harbour Bay where Columbus is said to have seen manatees for the first time, and mistaken them for mermaids. Little

Goat and Great Goat Islands lie offshore, and get their name from the custom of sailors leaving goats on easily accessible islands so there would be a fresh meat supply when they next sailed by. Little Goat was used by the US as a naval base for part of the Second World War.

North of Old Harbour is the **Little Ascot Race Course**, and just to the northwest are the ruins of **Colbeck Castle**. The house, at one time the largest on the island, is believed to have been built by Colonel John Colbeck, an officer in Cromwell's army that took the island in 1655.

MAY PEN

The road continues to **May Pen**, the main town of the parish of Clarendon. Many of the towns and villages have the name Pen, and this denotes that they have grown from farms where livestock was kept in pens. From Old Harbour you can take the coastal road that runs south from Freetown to Salt River to Lionel Town. You can then explore the promontory as far as Mahoe Garden, and visit the **Portland Lighthouse**. Carlisle Bay lies to the west of the promontory and there is a nice beach at **Jackson Bay** that is part of it. You can then take the B12 north back into May Pen past Hayes and the quarries on the right and then Halse Hall Great House on the left, or through Alley and Race Course on the more westerly secondary road which rejoins the B12 just south of town at Curatoe Hill. **Alley** used to be an important producer of indigo and the surrounding Vere area was so prosperous that it had its own parish status. The former parish church of St Peter's in Alley was built in

1715 and is noted for its organ.

From May Pen continue on the A2 past the Denbeigh Agricultural Showgrounds to Four Paths and Toll Gate where the road splits. The B12 runs off to the left back down to the coast to Rest. Just south of Rest is the **Milk River Spa** at Milk River Bath, which has the highest naturally occurring radioactive water in the world. The water is very warm as it comes out of the ground and is said to have great therapeutic powers. From Rest you can get down to the small Farquhars Beach. It then runs along the south coast past Long Bay (not to be confused with Long Bay on the east coast, south of Boston) and Old Woman's Point to Alligator. You can then head north again to reconnect with the A2 at Gutters, south of Mandeville.

MANDEVILLE

Our route continues along the A2 through **Porus**, at the center of an important citrus growing area, into sprawling Mandeville. It was named after Lord Mandeville, the eldest son of the Duke of Manchester, the Governor after whom the parish is named. Manchester parish is the island's largest producer of bauxite, a red ore. This explains the red soil seen throughout the parish.

Mandeville is the chief town of Manchester parish, Jamaica's mountain resort, the island's largest hill town and the fifth largest urban center. The town was laid out in 1816 and many of the original buildings can still be seen. Although only 64 miles (103km) from Kingston, Mandeville has a charm – and a climate – all of its own, as if it has been sheltered against all the developments in the capital and around the coast. It has a town square, parish church and clock tower, and many large, elegant early nineteenth-century houses to see along the winding streets. The square is more like a village green and Mandeville has been described as the most English town on Jamaica.

It is now a tourist center with delightful and charming hotels and guesthouses, and the market town for the surrounding rich agricultural areas. You can buy a wide variety of fruit and nuts for a picnic from the roadside stalls. It is also a service center for the two nearby bauxite works.

Origin of the Ortanique

The year round good weather brings out the best in Mandeville's amateur gardens, and the annual Spring Flower Show is well worth visiting. One of the town's claims to fame is as the place where the juicy ortanique was cultivated. This unique Jamaican fruit was developed in the 1920s by C. P. Jackson, and gets its name because it is part orange, part tangerine and unique.

Examples of the splendid architecture of Spanish Town

Mandeville Hotel

EATING OUT

• IN AND AROUND MANDEVILLE AND THE SOUTH COAST•

Restaurants are graded $ inexpensive, $$ moderate, $$$ expensive

Bamboo Village $-$$

Chinese, Ward Plaza,
☎: 926-4515

Country Fresh $$

Home cooking Jamaican, Astra
Country Inn, ☎: 962-3265

Golf View $-$$

Jamaican-International, Golf View
Hotel, ☎: 962-4471

Manchester Arms Pub and Restaurant $$-$$$

Jamaican-Continental,
Mandeville Hotel, ☎: 962-9764

Villa Bella $$-$$$

Jamaican and great breakfasts,
Villa Bella Hotel, ☎: 964-2243

Willows, $$

Local-International, Invercauld
Great House and Hotel,
☎: 965-2750

Mandeville Square and Green are the heart of the town and surrounded by most of the oldest buildings. The Court House was built in the 1820s from locally hewn limestone blocks. Beside it is the former rectory, the oldest building in the town which over the years has been an inn, guesthouse and is now a private house. The Parish Church also dates from the early 1820s, while the **Mandeville Hotel** on Hotel Street is a town landmark. It was built as a barracks for English troops, later became the Officers' Quarters and Mess, and in 1875 changed to a hotel. The Information Centre is at the Astra Inn on Ward Avenue, beyond the Tudor Theatre, and the Sugar Industry Research Institute is to the north off Kendal Road. There is a S.W.A. Craft Centre close to the Manchester shopping plaza, and the town market, just south of the square, sells fruit and vegetables, fresh fish and meat, including goat heads that are considered a delicacy.

The railway station is just to the north at **Williamsfield** where there is also the small **High Mountain coffee factory** and the **Pioneer Chocolate factory** ☎: 963-4216, both of which can be visited. There are tours of the Coffee Factory where you can see the whole coffee process from the roasting of the beans to grinding and packing. By appointment ☎: 963-4211.

Places to Visit

In and around Mandeville

Marshall's Pen
☎: 963-8569.

Ostrich Park at Lacovia
☎: 997-6555.

YS Falls
The falls can be visited from 9.30am to 4.15pm Tuesday to Sunday ☎: 997-6055. South Coast Safaris ☎: 965-2513,and St Elizabeth Safaris ☎: 965-2374, run boat tours of the Black River and trips to the YS Falls from Black River town, daily between 9am and 3.30pm. Tours leave from the old rum warehouse jetty for the 7 mile (11km) guided tour.

Maggotty Falls and the Apple Valley Park
☎: 997-6000

Glenwyn Halt
☎: 997-6036

Appleton Estate
There are tours of the distillery and tasting, daily between 10.30am to 6pm ☎: 963-2210.

Black River Spa
☎: 965-2255

Mayfield Ranch
☎: 965-6234

Mayfield Falls
☎: 888-974-8000

OTHER THINGS TO SEE AND DO IN AND AROUND MANDEVILLE.

The massive *Alcan Kirkvine* bauxite works are to the north east, and tours can be arranged. The *Cecil Charlton Mansion* is a mile and a half (2.5km) south of town on Huntingdon Summit. The unusual octagonal house looks out over pastures and corals with grazing cattle and horses, and there are aviaries in the garden.

About 10 miles (16km) north of Mandeville is the delightful hill town of **Christiana**. It is remarkably well preserved, the churches date from the mid-1800s and there are many fine old buildings. If visiting this market town, visit **Hotel Villa Bella**, a hill top plantation surrounded by citrus trees and coffee plants. You can enjoy traditional English tea on the verandah which offers stunning panoramic views, eat in the excellent restaurant, or stay overnight in one of the delightful rooms.

You can also visit the **Magic Toy Factory**, which produces all wood toys and souvenirs. The **Gourie Recreation Centre** is just north of Christiana on the B5 and offers many hiking trails and the Gourie Cave the source of the Black River. Grove Place has the island's largest livestock breeding research station. It is to the northwest on the B6 and further up the road is **Mile Gully** that has a pretty nineteenth century church.

The Paul Cross Nursery, on Manchester Road, near Newleight Road, was started by a New Jersey Catholic priest as a self-help project.

Plants produced, mostly anthuriums, are mainly exported to the US. There is a charming courtyard area with lily pond and a large variety of orchids. You can also visit by appointment the gardens of Carmen Stephenson off New Green Road. She specializes in orchids, anthuriums and ortaniques.

The beautiful grounds of the 120 year-old **Manchester Club**, off Caledonia Road, host championship golf and tennis tournaments during July. The 9-hole course is the Island's and the Caribbean's oldest, with a very English feel about it.

Marshall's Pen is an eighteenth-century Great House on a 300-acre (120-hectares) cattle ranch and wildlife sanctuary. The former coffee plantation was bought by Arthur Sutton in 1939 and is now famous for rearing Red Poll calves. The present owner, Robert Sutton, is one of the Island's leading ornithologists, and there are birding tours of the estate and almost 100 different species have been recorded. The estate can be visited by appointment only.

Shooter's Hill offers great panoramic views, and just to the east,

Treasure Beach

Above: Negril, waters end
Right: Negril Lighthouse

Treasure Beach

close to the junctions of routes B4, B5 and B6 is the Pickappeppa factory, which produces a piquant pepper sauce, not unlike Worcestershire sauce, which is exported worldwide. Bill Laurie's Steak House is rated one of the best in the Caribbean and overlooks Mandeville. It also has a museum of antique cars, carriages and license plates from all over the word. The area offers the chance for hiking, horse riding, birding and camping.

ON ALONG THE SOUTH COAST

From Mandeville the A2 runs to Spur Tree, the site of Marlborough Great House, built in 1795 in Palladian style, and then on to Wilton and Santa Cruz. It then runs along a stretch of highway known as Bamboo Avenue to Middle Quarters. For almost three miles (5km) the towering bamboo forms a gently swaying tunnel. As this is a very popular scenic drive, there are the attendant vendors along the roadside, and if you are feeling hungry, you can snack on delicious shrimps.

You can also visit one of Jamaica's newest attractions, the **Ostrich Park** at **Lacovia**. This 100-acre (40-hectare) working ostrich farm also features a collection of exotic birds, petting zoo, horseback riding and a food pavilion.

There are a number of trips into the interior that can be taken here. It is worth taking the short detour north here on the B6 to YS (really Wyess, but almost always written as YS), north of Middle Quarters, to visit the **YS Falls** set in 2,000 acres (800-hecatres) of pastureland. The seven waterfalls cascade down about 120ft (37m) into the YS River that then runs south into the Black River.

Black River Safari Tour

Gernman Origins

You can continue north on the B6 to visit **Seaford Town**. The area was settled by a group of Germans from Bremen in the 1830s and within ten years, more than 1,500 had moved into the settlement thanks to land grants made available by Lord Seaford. He donated 500 acres of his Westmoreland Estate to encourage European immigrants. Each settler was given a small parcel of land, mostly forest that had to be cleared. Most of the families still have German names and there is a small museum about their history near the Catholic Church.

From YS take the right hand fork, still the B6, to **Maggotty** with the Maggotty Falls and the Apple Valley Park, in the center of town with fishing ponds and rods for hire, boating, trails, waterfalls and camping. Also visit **Glenwyn Halt**, on the riverbank just outside town with its thatched huts and local arts and crafts.

In **Appleton** you must visit the Appleton Estate that produces what many people consider to be the world's finest rum. From Maggotty you can continue north through Retirement to visit the **Accompong Maroon Village**, although if you are continuing round the coast to Montego Bay, it is perhaps better to take an organized tour from there.

Return to the A2 that then runs south to the fishing village of Black River with its bright gingerbread houses along the water's edge. The town used to be a busy port, noted for the export of timber, sugar and honey. There is a popular produce market on Friday and Saturday. The Black River is the longest in Jamaica and one of the haunts of the rare Jamaica crocodile. It runs to the sea on the left hand side of the road through a marshy area. The Waterloo Guest House in Black River was the first property in Jamaica to have electric lights, and if you want to relax you can bathe in the Black River Spa or the nearby Crane Beach.

From Black River you can drive south east through Watchwell to quiet **Treasure Beach** where you can watch the fishermen in the village at one end of this beautiful south coast beach in the parish of St Elizabeth. Treasure Beach really consists of four small bays, which in order from the north are Billys, Frenchmans, Calabash and Great Pedro. There are many walking trails in the area, especially around Great Bluff. You can eat at Jakes, or the Yabba Restaurant or Old Wharfe Restaurant, both at the Treasure Beach Hotel and offering Jamaican cuisine. The road then continues a short distance to **Southfield**, where you can ride at the Mayfield Ranch. You can take an exciting cycle trip or hike with Bike Mountain Water Fall Tours to visit Mayfield Falls.

Continue to Yardley Chase where the road runs out near Lover's Leap. According to legend, the 1,500ft 457m) sheer cliffs got their name because two young slaves who had fallen in love, jumped to their deaths rather than be split up. There are great scenic views along the south coast from the sheer cliffs that plunge to the sea. The area is open from 9am to 5pm daily.

The island tour continues along the

A2 which runs along the coast through Whitehouse and **Bluefields**, both of which have fine beaches, to Savanna-la-Mar, where the A2 ends. There is an early morning fish market at **Whitehouse**, and in 1670 adventurer Henry Morgan sailed from Bluefields for Panama where he achieved notoriety by sacking the city.

Savanna La Mar has literally had a stormy existence, and has been hit several times by hurricanes. In 1748 ships sheltering in the bay in the shelter of Cabrita Point were driven by the winds onto the beach and wrecked. The town was almost totally flattened by a hurricane in 1780 and during a hurricane in 1912 the schooner Laconia was dumped in the middle of the main street. Today it lies rotting in the bay.

The locals have long used the fort as a swimming pool, and if you look over the walls into the water you can see a large cannon resting on the seabed. When you arrive at the fort, you may come across Moses, the self-appointed guide, who has a fund of interesting information in return for an appropriate tip. The town is unusual in that it is almost entirely built along the sprawling Great George Street that runs for one mile (1.6km) to the fort on the waterfront.

NEGRIL AND THE WESTERN COAST

Negril is the main resort area on the island's west coast, and extends from the nineteenth-century Negril Lighthouse in the parish of Westmoreland in the south, to *Bloody Bay* in Hanover Parish in the north. Bloody Bay gets its name because it used to be a whaling station and whales would be hauled on to the beach to be cut up for their blubber. The Negril Bay waters are shallow and protected by the offshore reef. The coastline takes in seven miles (11km) of white sand beach, which centuries ago was used by pirates to bring their captured treasure ashore.

Calico Jack Rackham

Calico Jack Rackham, the most notorious pirate in Jamaica's history, was taken prisoner at Negril Beach in 1702 while landing on the beach with Anne Bonney and Mary Read, two of his female crew. Calico Jack got his nickname because of his preference for Calico underwear. He was tried for piracy and hanged, and his body left on display in an iron frame. The two women both claimed to be pregnant so were spared death, but spent some time in prison.

EATING OUT

The following symbols are used:
$ inexpensive, $$ moderate,
$$$ expensive.

Beach Comber $$
Italian, ☎: 957-4170

Café Au Lait $$
French-Jamaican and good wine list,
Mirage Resort, ☎: 957-4471

Captain's Table $$-$$$
Continental-Caribbean, Poinciana
Beach, ☎: 957-4100

Charela Inn $$
Jamaican-Continental, Charela Inn,
☎: 957-4277

Char Grill $-$$
Seafood-Jamaican, Xtabi Resort,
☎: 957-4336

Chez Maurice $$-$$$
Seafood-Italian, Hotel Samsara,
☎: 957-4395

Chuckles $
Jamaican, Chuckles, ☎: 957-4250

Coconut Palm $-$$
Caribbean, Negril Cabins Resort,
☎: 957-5350

Coral Seas Beach $-$$
Italian, Coral Seas Beach,
☎: 957-9226

Coral Seas Cliff $$
Seafood-Jamaican, ☎: 957-3147

Cosmo's Seafood $$
Seafood-Jamaican, Norman Manley
Boulevard, ☎: 957-4330

Country Country Beach Bar and Grill, $$
Seafood and grill, Country Country
☎: 957-4273

Country Restaurant $$
Vegetarian, Country Resort Cottages,
☎: 957-4273

Erica's Café $$-$$$
Seafood and lobster specialities,
☎: 957-4322

Feathers $$
Pasta-Italian, Swept Away Resort,
reservations recommended,
☎: 957-4061

Fun Holiday Beach $$
Seafood, Norman Manley Boulevard,
☎: 957-3585

Gambino's $$
Italian, Beachcomber Hotel,
☎: 957-4171

Happy Bananas $$
English pub fare, West End,
☎: 957-0871

Hibiscus Dining Room $$
Jamaican-Continental, T-Water
Beach Hotel, ☎: 957-4270

Hungry Lion $-$$
Vegetarian-Seafood, West End,

Kaiser's Cafe $-$$
Jamaican, Lighthouse Road,
☎: 957-4070

Kuyaba on the Beach $-$$
Jamaican, Kuyaba on the Beach,
☎: 957-4318

Lion's Head Gallery $-$$
Jamaican-continental,
Bar-B-Barn Hotel, ☎: 957-4267

Man Friday's Patio $-$$
Jamaican, Foote Prints, ☎: 957-4300

Margueritaville $$

Sports bar and all day grill, 52 different margueritas, Norman Manley Blvd, ☎: 957-4467

Mariner's Inn $$

Seafood-Jamaican,Mariner's Inn, ☎: 957-4348

Merrils $$

Seafood-grill, Merrils Beach Resort, ☎: 957-4741

Negril Tree House $$

Jamaican, Negril Tree House, ☎: 957-4287

Orchard Terrace $$

Jamaican-International, Negril Gardens, ☎: 957-4408

Paradise Garden Café $$

Italian, Point Village, ☎: 957-5170

Paradise Yard $$

Mexican-Rasta, Savanna-la-Mar Road, ☎: 957-4006

Pickled Parrot $$

American-Jamaican, West End Road, ☎: 957-4336

Rick's Cafe $$-$$$

Jamaican-Continental, voted one of the world's top ten bars, Cliffside dining and cliff diving, West End, ☎: 957-0380

Robinson Crusoe $$-$$$

Seafood, Foote Prints, ☎: 957-4300

Rock Cliff $-$$

Jamaica-International, Rock Cliffs Hotel, ☎: 957-4331

Rockhouse $$-$$$

New Jamaican cuisine, Rockhouse Hotel, ☎: 957-4373

Rondel Village Restaurant $-$$

Jamaican-American, Rondel Village, ☎: 957-4403

Runaway Jamaican

Runaway Bay, ☎: 973-2671

Seething Cauldron $$

Seafood-Jamaican, Negril Beach Club, ☎: 957-4220

Silver Sand $$

Jamaican-International, Silver Sand Hotel, ☎: 957-4207

Summerset Village $-$$

Seafood-Jamaican, Summerset Village, ☎: 957-4409

Tanya's $$

European-Nouvelle Jamaican, Sea Splash Resort, ☎: 957-4041

Unda de Thatch $-$$

Jamaican-International, Chuckles, ☎: 957-4250

Vendome $$-$$$

French-Jamaican, Charela Inn, ☎: 957-4277

Village Connection $$

Jamaican, Point Village Resort, ☎: 957-5170

Xtabi $$

Seafood, West End, ☎: 957-4336

Then continue west through London to Negril.

Negril is very popular and has grown rapidly in recent years. Most of this stems from the early 1960s when new roads and drainage canals were built, and it was then 'discovered' by the hippies who set up a colony. Their easy-going attitude remains today throughout the town that stretched for miles along the bay. Resort development is supposed to be carefully controlled, and no building by law is allowed to be taller than the tallest palm. Apart from the beautiful beaches, the waters offer world-class diving and a wealth of watersports.

The tourist office, is in the Adrija Plaza De Negril, with the post office, police station and Negril Yacht Club further along West End Road, and the two-floor crafts market almost opposite on Lighthouse Road, where there is Island clothing, woodcarvings and local crafts. It opens early and closes late!

The Anancy Family Fun and Nature Park on bustling Norman Manley Boulevard, has an 18-hole miniature golf course, go kart rides, mini-train, fishing pond, nature trail and three small museums.

Because of the rapid resort development, you are likely to be hustled in Negril. Ignore the hustlers and enjoy the town. Its location on the west coast of the Island, means there are fabulous sunsets. The town boasts many fine resorts but you should try and check out the foyer of the Grand Lido with its marble reception area, waterfalls and Tiffany glass chandeliers. The hotel also boasts the 147ft (45m) motor yacht Zein, which was the wedding gift from Aristotle Onassis to Prince Rainier of Monaco and Grace Kelly and used for their honeymoon. It is now used for sunset cruises.

Opposite the Grand Lido is Hedonism 11, another Superclubs Resort where the bars and discos stay open to dawn.

Booby Cay, the island at the northern end of the beach, was used during the filming of Walt Disney's film *'Twenty Thousand Leagues Under The Sea'*, and for some scenes from the James Bond film *'Thunderball'*. **Negril Lighthouse**, at the southern end of the bay, is the tallest structure in Negril at 100ft (30m) above sea level. It can be visited daily between 9am and 4pm. There are good views here of the **West End Cliffs** where cliff diving and sunset watching are popular pastimes.

Much of the area inland is a huge marsh with mangroves and a wealth of water birds. There are also cruises (☎: 957-4323) to **Negril's Reef** with visits to nearby coral islands, such as Booby Cay. Another mini-trip is to visit **Whitehall Great House**, ten minutes away, on a former 300-acre (129-hectare) pimento plantation. The great house was built by slaves at the end of the seventeenth century, but was damaged by fire in 1985 and has not been repaired. The estate is noted for a giant cottonwood tree reputed to be 900 years old and is the resting place of Robert Parkinson, who discovered the disease named after him. It is open daily.

Places to Visit

Negril Galleries

Gallery Hoffstead
Plaza de Negril, ☎: 956-2241

Geraldine Robins
West End Road (unlisted number)

Kool Brown
West End Road, ☎: 957-4361

Le Bric a Brac
Negril Beach, ☎: 957-4277

Patrick Weise Studio Gallery
West End Road, ☎: 957-4456

Negril and the Western Coast

The tourist office
☎: 957-4243

The Anancy Family Fun and Nature Park
☎: 957-5100.

Negril Lighthouse,
Can be visited daily between 9am and 4pm.

Whitehall Great House
Open daily.

LUCEA TO MONTEGO BAY

To most people this stretch of coastline is what the Caribbean is all about and what the perfect tropical beach should look like. Coral reefs off shore provide safe swimming in the clear, warm waters, the golden sand beaches are fringed with gently swaying palms that provide shade, and there are street stalls and beach bars providing Jamaican fast food, snacks and drinks.

Lucea, once a flourishing sugar port, still has a fine natural harbor and is a charming little town. It is the chief town of Hanover parish, and you can visit the eighteenth-century Fort Charlotte that stands on a promontory overlooking the harbor, the parish church with its steeple, and interesting tombstones in the cemetery. The nineteenth-century Court House has a clock tower modeled after the helmet once worn by the German Royal Guard. The clock was made in 1817 and it is thought that the 'helmet' tower was sent by mistake but having arrived was erected anyway. Between Lucea and Sandy Bay there are miles of coastal mangrove swamps which are rich in bird and marine life.

At **Kenilworth** there are the ruins of one of the best examples of old industrial architecture in Jamaica, including the remains of a sugar mill and distillery.

MONTEGO BAY

Montego Bay, or Mo Bay as it is popularly known, is deservedly one of the most famous tourist destinations in the world. Over the years it has attracted the rich and the famous, and been the haunt of royalty. Many of their luxury villas still grace the hills with fabulous sea views. The bay offers wonderful beaches and the town has lots to offer. The town of Montego Bay is divided into two distinct areas, the residential and the tourist. The former is largely to the south of Sam Sharpe Square and west of St James Street until its junction with Barnett Street. The main tourist part of town, packed with vendors, stalls, higglers and hustlers, is east of Sam Sharpe Square nearer the waterfront, and most of the main resorts and hotels are to the north, between the town and the Sir Donald Sangster International Airport, or east of it.

Today, Montego Bay is Jamaica's second city with its international airport and modern cruise ship pier that make it the tourism capital of the north coast. It has four championship golf courses close by, and boasts one of the Island's most beautiful beaches at Doctors' Cave.

There are more guest rooms in and around Montego Bay than anywhere else on the Island, and some of the most luxurious private villas in the Caribbean. There are several all-inclusive luxury resorts, plenty of nightlife and a number of special weekly events. These include the Cornwall Beach Party, an Evening on the Great River – a torchlight ride in dugout canoes followed by dinner, dancing and entertainment – and MoBay Monday Night Out, an evening of traditional folk music and dancing and island fare.

A SHORT WALKING TOUR OF MONTEGO BAY

Sam Sharpe Square in the heart of Montego Bay makes a good place to start a walking tour of the town. The square, formerly called Charles Square, contains a collection of bronze statues sculpted by island-born Kay Sullivan that show the Bible-thumping Sam Sharpe talking to four of his followers. The stone Cage is the other main feature of the square. **The Cage** was built in 1806 and originally used to hold captured runaway slaves and sailors, and those out after Curfew. Since then it has been a town lock-up, latrine, a clinic and a tourist office. It now houses a small museum. The square is still used for political and other local meetings, and it and the surrounding narrow streets, are filled with vendors selling everything from fresh produce and T-shirts to arts and crafts.

Opposite page: Montego Bay from Richmond heights

Doctors Cave Beach

Sangster International Airport

MONTEGO BAY

N
W — E
S

Upper King St

Post Office ★

The Cage

Sam Sharp Square

Union St

Perry St

Market St

MONTEGO

BAY

Church St

Prince St

Water La

The Court House

St James St

Orange St

Payne st

Queen St

Duke St

Craft Market

Strand St

Harbour St

Hart St

Cottage Rd

Fish La

Gregg La

Barnet St

Corinaldi Ave

Jarrett Park

Barnet La

Tate St

Railway La

Thomson St

McCarty St

River Bay Ave

Green Ave

Fustic St

Montego River

★ Cruise Dock
★ Yacht Club
★ Bob Marley Performance Centre

Mistaken Enemy

Head north on St James Street past the main post office and library, both on your left, then Fort Street to the ruins of Fort Montego (also known as Fort Frederick) that guard the inner harbor. The fort did not see any serious action although in 1760 one of the cannon blew up during a victory volley to celebrate the surrender of Havana, and in 1794 the fort opened fire on what it thought was a hostile French ship, only to discover it was an English schooner. Fortunately, the gunners missed their target. You can still visit the gun battery with its three cannon and the powder magazine. The Fort Montego crafts market is located here.

Inland from the fort is the area known as Canterbury, a densely packed shantytown, and a stark contrast to the homes of the wealthy to be seen on the hills above the town. Gloucester Avenue, along the waterfront, has many of the duty-free shops.

Head back into town and at the roundabout take Cooke Boulevard that runs along the waterfront to the Parish Wharf. Two blocks inland from Parish Wharf is Strand Street and the Strand Theatre. The Crafts Market is in Harbour Street beside the bay with The Creek running inland just to the south of it. The mini-bus terminal is alongside the craft market. The small promontory just south of the creek is Gun Point Wharf, and beyond that

are the banana wharves, and across the bay is the cruise ship dock on the man-made Freeport peninsula, which is also the home of the **Montego Bay Yacht Club**, and the **Bob Marley Performing Centre**. The area was reclaimed from the sea in the 1960s, by a combination of dredging and infill.

If you follow the road by the Creek inland, you meet Barnett Street that runs southeast out of town. The railway station is off Barnett Street in Railway Lane, and a little beyond in Fustic Street is the produce market.

Continue up Creek Street to the junction with Dome Street to visit **the Dome**. The structure was built in 1837 over the creek that used to supply the town with water. The Keeper of the Creek had his office and living accommodation on the first floor.

Continue along Dome Street and turn right into Prince Street, where at the end of the road there is a path to the 82-foot (25m) deep **Brandon Hill Cave**.

Return to Dome Street and turn right to its junction with Union Street. Just before the junction on the right is the Montego Bay High School, and round the corner in Union Street, on the right just before East Street is the old **Slave Ring**. Originally used to sell slaves, it later became one of the island's most popular cock fight rings. Turn left into East Street then right into Church Street then left into Payne Street for the parish church, back near the square.

St James Parish Church was started in 1775 and dedicated in 1778, and is regarded as one of the finest on the island. It was almost completely destroyed by an

Montego Bay Marine Park

In May 1990 the Montego Bay Marine Park was established covering more than 9 sq miles (15.3 sq km), and stretching from the Donald Sangster International Airport to the Great River. The park covers a number of different marine environments which can be visited and studied, and allows watersports in designated areas. Its purpose is to preserve and manage Montego Bay's marine resources for the benefit and enjoyment of the people of Jamaica as well as visitors to the island. The marine resources include the coral reefs, seagrass beds, mangrove wetlands, and all the fish, conch, lobster and other plants and animals living in the sea or along the shore line. Mooring buoys have been located at leading dive sites to reduce anchor damage to the coral reefs.

earthquake in 1957 but has been faithfully restored to its original appearance. The graveyard contains several elaborate tombs of planters.

Montego Bay has several art galleries, including the **Gallery of West Indian Art** and the **Bay Gallery**. Other shopping opportunities include rum and island liquors, perfumes, glassware, English cashmere and local arts and crafts. There is also shopping at Freeport.

The **Burchell Memorial Church** was established in 1824 by the Rev. Thomas Burchell, a Baptist missionary and outspoken abolitionist. Most of the early congregation were slaves, and Sam Sharpe was a deacon there.

OTHER THINGS TO SEE AND DO AT MONTEGO BAY

The Barnett Estate Plantation offers a range of activities, including jitney tours of the historic sugar, banana and mango plantation. There are tropical gardens featuring native flora and fauna, and fine dining at the restored Sugar Mill. The estate covers 3,000-acres (1200-hectares) and stretches from

the sea to the mountains and offers great views over Montego Bay. There are guided tours of the Great House that contains a wealth of memorabilia about the many famous people who have entertained in the house over the past three centuries. The estate has been owned and run by the Kerr-Jarretts, one of Jamaica's oldest families for 11 generations. Colonel Nicholas Jarrett came to Jamaica in 1655 with the British army to take the Island from Spain.

The Belvedere Estate offers tours of the 1,000-acre (400-hecatare) working estate. The heritage tour with guides in period costumes, includes 14 delightful houses, each used for a different purpose, and explanations of bush medicine. There is also citrus and herb farming and the old sugar mill.

Blue Hole Museum is in the hills 6 miles (10km) from Montego Bay. The museum's exhibits include a reconstruction of an Arawak village, and there is a mini-zoo. There are tours of the eighteenth century Great House.

(Continued on page 88)

When Columbus first landed on Jamaica he anchored further east in Discovery Bay. After four days he started to explore westwards and sailed into Montego Bay where he was able to pick up winds to sail back to Cuba. Because of this he named the bay Golfo de Buen Tiempo, meaning the Gulf of Good Weather. In the early-seventeenth century, it was renamed by Spanish sailors who anchored offshore to collect cargoes of lard. The early estates rendered animal fat, from their own cattle and slain wild pigs, to produce lard that was used aboard for cooking. The Spanish word for lard is manteca, and Montego Bay first appeared on Spanish maps as Manterias in 1655. Ten years later the island was in British hands and the parish of St James was established, although there was no settlement at Montego Bay because pirates raided the coast, and hostile Maroons occupied the interior. The town developed in the late-1700s, and became a major shipping port for sugar cane and later bananas, and many of the estate owner's fine great houses, such as Greenwood and Rose Hall can still be seen on the outskirts of town. It was the scene of Jamaica's most important slave uprising. It took place over the winter of 1832-3 and started at the Kensington Estate, about five miles inland to the southeast. It was led by Baptist Samuel (Sam) Sharpe who was an outspoken opponent of slavery and it should have been a peaceful sit-in over Christmas. Some of his supporters, however, broke into the plantation's rum store, got drunk and set fire to buildings and the cane fields. Slaves on other plantations joined in and it spread to Montego Bay. The revolt took several months to crush and Sharpe was hanged in the square, but it did sow the seeds for Emancipation that was granted by the British Parliament two years later.

The area's first hotel opened in 1924 and as agriculture has declined, tourism has taken over as the main industry and employer.

Opposite page: White sands of Montego Bay

Above: Rose Hall

Left: Lush Vegetation of Montego Bay

Below: Sam Sharpe Square, Down Town Montego Bay

The following symbols are used:
$ inexpensive, $$ moderate,
$$$ expensive.

Akbars $$

Indian, Gloucester Avenue,
☎: 979-0133

Ambrosia $$-$$$

Mediterranean, Rose Hall,
☎: 953-2650

Atrium $$

Continental-Jamaican, Morgan Road,
☎: 953-2605

Banana Walk
Restaurant $$-$$$

International, Seawind Beach Resort,
☎: 979-8070

Belfield 1794 $$-$$$

Jamaican-Caribbean, Barnett Estate,
☎: 952-2382

Brewery $-$$

Pub fare, Miranda Ridge,
☎: 940-2613

Calabash $-$$

Jamaican ☎: 952-3891

Cascade Room $$

Seafood-Jamaican, Gloucester
Avenue, ☎: 952-3171

Castles $-$$

3 restaurants offering grill, à la carte
and buffet, Sand Castles,
☎: 953-3250

Coconut Grove $$

Jamaican-Italian, Doctor's cave
Beach Hotel, ☎: 952-4355

Crusoe's $$-$$$

Caribbean, Wyndham Rose Hall
Resort, ☎: 953-2650

Day-O Plantation
Restaurant $$

Seafood-Jamaican, Fairfield,
☎: 952-1825

Diplomat $$-$$$

Open-air Continental, Queens Drive,
☎: 952-3353

Dolphin Grill $$-$$$

Seafood-Continental, Rose Hall,
☎: 953-2676

Dunn's Villa $$

Jamaican specialties, close to the
Wyndham Hotel, ☎: 953-7459

Fish n' Bits $$

Seafood, Jamaica Grandiosa Resort,
☎: 979-3205

Fountain Terrace $$

Italian Seawind Beach Resort,
☎: 979-8070

Georgian House $$

Jamaican-Continental, Orange
Street, ☎: 952-0632

Great House Verandah
$$-$$$

Elegant candlelit dining, Tryall Club,
☎: 956-5660

Greenhouse $-$$

Jamaican-fast food, Gloucester
Avenue, ☎: 952-7838

Guangzhou $$

Chinese, Miranda Ridge Plaza,
☎: 952-6200

Houseboat $$

Candlelit fondue, anchored off
Montego Freeport, ☎: 979-8854

Il Giardino $$-$$$

Excellent Italian, Half Moon Hotel,
☎: 953-2211

Jamaka-Mi-Krazy $-$$

Jamaican-seafood, on the beach 10 miles (16km) from Montego Bay, ☎: 956-5448

Julia's $$

Italian overlooking the bay, ☎: 952-1772

King Arthur's

Seafood and Continental Rose Hall, ☎: 953-2022

La Scala $$-$$$

Italian, Holiday Inn, ☎: 953-2480

Luna di Mare $$-$$$

Italian fine dining, Wyndham Rose Hall Resort, ☎: 953-2650

Lychee Gardens $$

Chinese, East Street, ☎: 952-9428

Margueritaville Sports Bar and Grill, $-$$

Hot night spot, fast food grill, roof top hot tub, Gloucester Avenue, ☎: 952-4777

Marguerite's By The Sea $$

Seafood-Continental, Gloucester Avenue, ☎: 952-4777

The Native $$

Innovative Jamaican, Queen's Drive, ☎: 979-2769

Pelican $-$$

Jamaican-International, Gloucester Avenue, ☎: 952-3171

Pier 1 $$

Seafood-Continental, on the waterfront, ☎: 952-2452

Pork Pit $-$$

Jamaican, Kent Avenue, ☎: 952-1046 Richmond Hill $$ Seafood-Continental, Richmond Hill Inn, ☎: 952-3859

Ristorante Il Giardino $$

Italian-European, Half Moon Beach Club, ☎: 953-2211

Rite Stuff Cafe $

Fast food-ice cream Westgate Plaza, 952-3199

Royal Stocks $$

English pub fare and steakhouse, Half Moon Shopping Village, ☎: 953-9770

Seagrape Terrace $$-$$$

Nouvelle Caribbean, Half Moon Beach Club, ☎: 953-2211

Seaview Terrace $$

Seafood-Jamaican-Continental, Holiday Inn, ☎: 953-2485

Tapas $$

Spanish-Arabic, behind Coral Cliff Hotel, ☎: 952-2988

Taste of Jamaica $$

Exotic West Indian, Half Moon Village Plaza, ☎: 953-2576

Tony's Pizza $-$$

Pizza, Fantasy Arcade, ☎: 952-6365

Top O'The Bay $$

Seafood-Jamaican, Montego Bay Club Resort, ☎: 952-4310

Tower Restaurant $$

Jamaican, Seawind Beach Resort Village, ☎: 979-8070

Town House $$-$$$

Seafood-Continental, Church Street, ☎: 952-2660

Accompong Maroon Tours

All day tours to visit the Maroons in Cockpit Country. 8am. Tuesday, Thursday, and Saturday
☎: 952-3539

Appleton Express

Air-conditioned bus ride from Montego Bay to the Appleton Distillery including tour of Ipswich Caves and the distillery. 8.30am to 4pm Tuesday to Thursday
☎: 952-6606

Aquasol Theme Park

A $20 million attraction themed around the sun and the sea. It has great water attractions including a giant water slide, bathing and sunning areas, go-karting, restaurant, sports bar and nightclub.
☎: 940-1344.

The Barnett Estate Plantation

It is open for tours daily from 9am to 5.30pm, and in the evening for dining and entertainment.
☎: 952-2382.

The Belvedere Estate

It is open from 10am to 4pm, Monday to Saturday ☎: 952-6001.

Blue Hole Museum

It is open daily 9am to 4pm.
☎: 995-2070

Boonoonoonoos Beach Party

Live reggae band, 3-course Jamaican dinner open bar and native floorshow. 7pm to 11 pm, Friday. Chester Castle Great House is 14 miles (23km) west in Hanover, and is set in 100 acres (80 hectares). There are all-day tours.

Tryall Water Wheel

Cockpit Country Tour

9.30am to 5.30pm, daily.
Coral See offers sunset parties and marine sanctuary cruises. The vessel has seating for 48 passengers who can see marine life through viewing windows six ft below the surface. She departs from Pier 1. ☎: 971-1049.

Cornwall Beach

This is the smallest of the public beaches in the area offering watersports and safe swimming. It is open daily from 9am to 5pm.

Croydon in The Mountains

A 132-acre (53 hectare) working plantation in Catadupa (45 minutes from Montego Bay). Its main crops are coffee, pineapples, plantains and citrus. Guided 1/2 day tour. 10:30am to 3pm, Tuesday, Wednesday and Friday ☎: 979-8267.

Doctor's Cave Beach

The beach is open 8.30am to 5.30pm, daily.
Evening on The Great River: Canoe trip up torch-lit river. Dinner, open bar music and folklore shows. 7pm to 11pm, Tuesday, Thursday and Sunday.

Hampden Great House Tour

Great House, rum distillery and factory tour Hilton High Day Tour: Conducted full day plantation tour including breakfast and lunch with an enjoyable Mento band. 7am to 3pm, Tuesday, Wednesday, Friday and Sunday ☎: 952-3343.

Hilton High Day Tours

Offer tethered hot air balloon rides from Montego Bay to St Leonard, a 360 acre (110hectare) private plantation ☎: 952-3343.

Jamaica Queen IV

A 61 foot (19m) double-decker, glass bottom power boat which offers day, sunset and dinner with dancing cruises ☎: 953-3392.

Lollypop by the Sea

Glass bottom boat ride with reggae band and dinner. Dancing on the beach. 7.30am to12.30pm, Wednesday.

Miskito Cove Beach Picnic

10am to 4pm, Tuesday and Thursday. Mountain Valley Rafting at Lethe 1 hour rafting trip on The Great River disembarking at scenic recreation area. An optional hayride and plantation tour is available. 9am to 5pm, daily ☎: 952-0527.

The Rocklands Bird Sanctuary at Anchovy

Bird feeding takes place daily at 3.15 p.m. You can watch or you can hand-feed the tame birds yourself.
☎: 952-2009.

Tryall Water Wheel

This gigantic water wheel is nearly 200 years old and still turning. The wheel was badly damaged during the 1832 uprising, and the date 1834 is thought to indicate when it was rebuilt. ☎: 956-5660.

Walter Fletcher Beach

Beach with lockers, changing rooms, snack counter, gift shops and boat cruises. 9am to 5pm daily. Beach party Friday evenings with live reggae band, Jamaican dinner, open bar and native floor show 7 to 11pm.

Wyndham Rose Hall's Sugar Mill Fall's Water Park

The largest in the Caribbean with slides, tube rafting and pools.

Places to Visit

Montego Bay Galleries

Elgo's Art Gallery
Gloucester Avenue, ☎: 971-3310

Gallery of West Indian Art
Orango Lane, ☎: 952-4547

Gallery Hoffstead
Lucea
☎: 956-2241

Heaven's Art Gallery
2 Church Lane, ☎: 52-2852

Images
Half Moon Shopping Village,
☎: 953-9043

Keith Chandler
Rock Wharf, ☎: 954-3314

Neville Budhais Gallery
Main Road, Reading,
☎: 979-2568

Sun Art Gallery
Half Moon Shopping Village,
☎: 953-3455

Things Jamaican
Montego Bay, Airport
☎: 952-1936

Things Jamaican
44 Fort Street, ☎: 952-5605

Wassi Art
Holiday Inn Village, ☎: 953-2338

Doctor's Cave Beach: World famous white sand and clear water beach believed to be fed by mineral springs. In 1906 the beach was donated to the town by Dr Alexander McCatty, an advocate of the therapeutic benefits of sea bathing. The cave was demolished during a hurricane in 1932. The area just inland from the beach was used as a burial ground. There is excellent snorkeling around the offshore reef, and glass bottom boats can be hired.

Orange River Lodge is an eighteenth-century sugar estate, and a former cattle and citrus property. It is also a backpacker's paradise. The 980 acres (392 hectares) nestle in the hills about 25 miles (40km) south east of Montego Bay. The Great House overlooks the River Valley with guest rooms and hostel accommodation, as well as camping facilities. Activities offered range from walking, mountain hiking, birding and cycling to river bathing, swimming, canoeing and horseback riding.

The Rocklands Bird Sanctuary at Anchovy, just inland to the south, features Doctor bird hummingbirds, the national bird, and other species only found on the island. The sanctuary and feeding station are run by the very knowledgeable Lisa Salmon.

MONTEGO BAY TO PORT MARIA

The stretch of coast road (A1) east from Kingston passes a number of resorts and hotels between Mahoe Bay and Rose Hall, including Sandals Royal Caribbean, Caribbean Beach, Half Moon, The Palms and Wyndham Rose Hall Beach and Country Club.

Just inland from Little River is the magnificent stone **Rose Hall Great House**, which has been faithfully restored to its eighteenth-century Georgian elegance. Its white fronted facade is illuminated at night and looks splendid from a distance.

Continue east for about 5 miles (8km) from the turn off to another grand old house. Greenwood Great House is more than 200 years old, and was owned by the family of Elizabeth Barrett-Browning, the famous English poet. The museum

Ghost Story

Rose Hall Great Housereenwood Great House was said to have been the finest eighteenth century Great House in the Caribbean. Built between 1770 and 1780 by John Palmer, the representative of George 111, it was, according to legend, later the home of Annie Palmer, the beautiful 'White Witch', who moved there in 1820 and ruled with incredible cruelty before meeting a violent death. It is said she murdered all her three husbands, as well as numerous slave lovers, before being killed herself in bed by her slaves in 1833. In 1978 a huge crowd gathered as psychics tried to communicate with her ghost. One psychic was led to a large termite mound that was broken open and inside there was a brass urn containing a voodoo doll. It is a great story but there is no solid evidence to support it. Its present owner, US industrialist John Rollins, restored the house in the 1960's. He went to great lengths to re-furnish it authentically. The house contains antiques and art treasures from around the world, and is open from 9am to 6pm, daily ☎: 953-2323. There is a souvenir shop in the old dungeon and in Annie's Pub there are some intriguing photographs that seem to show a ghostly figure lurking in the background!

Above: Safari Village (near Falmouth), a popular location with film makers

Right James Bond Beach
Below: Falmouth Church

contains one of Jamaica's finest collections of antique furniture, musical instruments and maps. It is open daily from 9am to 6pm ☎: 953-1077.

The route then passes Flamingo Beach and Salt Marsh on **Half Moon Bay**. Visit the Half Moon Shopping Village with its world-class shopping, restaurants and galleries. It is also the home of the **Bob Marley Experience and Theatre** which presents a 30-minute biographic documentary on the performer every hour on the hour. ☎: 953-3946.

Then continue to the historic Georgian town of Falmouth.

Laid out in 1790, **Falmouth** is considered the best-preserved Georgian town on the island, thanks largely to the efforts of the Georgian Society. Although many of the original shingle roofs have been replaced with zinc and tin, it is still easy to visualize how the town must have been in its heyday when it was the busiest port on the north coast. Today, fishermen sit on the grass banks mending their nets, while donkeys and goats often mingle with the townsfolk and tourists in the streets.

The town's prosperity, based on sugar cane, was short lived and by the mid-nineteenth century it had lost most of its trade to the new rail-head at Montego Bay and the larger port and harbor at Kingston. Named after the Cornish port, Falmouth has many interesting old buildings, especially along Main Street, around Water Square and in Market Street, with its stone and wooden homes with elegant wrought iron balconies and Adam-style doorways and friezes. Main Street was used for the location of several of the scenes in the film *Papillon*, which starred Steve McQueen. Wednesday, Friday and Saturday are market days, Wednesday for fabrics, clothing and crafts, and Friday and Saturday for produce.

St Peter's Church, built in 1795, in Duke Street is the second oldest church in Jamaica and noted for its stained glass windows, and there are usually craftsmen's stalls in the church car park and nearby road. The old Courthouse dates from 1815, although it was burnt down about 10 years later.

Passionate Abolitionist

The William Knibb Presbyterian Church is named after one of the island's most passionate abolitionists. For years he preached that the slaves should be freed, and his sermons so angered the planters, that they referred to his church as 'Knibb's pestilential praying hole'. In 1834, however, when Emancipation finally arrived, hundreds of slaves flocked to the church to offer their thanks. It is said that during the ceremony, chains and shackles were buried in a coffin, inscribed with the words: 'Colonial Slavery – died July 31, 1834 aged 276 years'.

Barrett House was built by sugar millionaire Edward Barrett. It was one of the many homes owned on the island by the Barrett family, whose most famous member was writer Elizabeth Barrett Browning.

Things to do in the area include a visit to the nearby **Jamaica Safari**

Village, a crocodile exhibition and farm with Leah the lioness, snakes, mongoose, petting zoo and bird sanctuary.

Film Set

F ans of James Bond films will recognize this as the location of the famous scene from *Live and Let Die*, where the super spy escapes from an island by using the crocodiles in the water as steppingstones! The safari village was also used to film some of the scenes in *Papillon*. There are guided natural history tours 9am to 5pm, daily ☎: 954-3065.

Martha Brae used to be a Spanish settlement called Melilla, and was the largest town in the area before Falmouth was established. Its main claim to fame is the massive wooden waterwheel, the oldest in the Western Hemisphere. The wheel was used to pump fresh water to Falmouth, long before New York was receiving piped drinking water. Martha Braed, according to legend, was the daughter of an Arawak Chief. She was forced by the Spanish to lead them to a cave where they believed they would find gold. Having led them into the cave, she is said to have used her magical powers to divert the river into the cavern so that all the Spanish drowned. More likely, the town was named after the wife of a local estate owner, but even she was reputed to have been a witch.

Martha Brae Rafting ☎: 952-0889, offers a 75-minute river trip aboard 30-foot (9m) bamboo rafts that begins at Rafter's Village, 4 miles from Falmouth. The river trip passes the **Good Hope Estate**, which can be visited from Falmouth by taking the Good Hope Road. The elegant Great House on the Good Hope Estate was built in 1755 and has been carefully restored and refurbished, and has ten guest rooms, all with four-poster beds. Facilities include swimming pool,

EATING OUT

• IN AND AROUND FALMOUTH •

The following symbols are used: $ inexpensive, $$ moderate, $$$ expensive.

Cha Cha Cha Restaurant $-$$

Seafood-Jamaican, open all day, Rose's By The Sea ☎: 954-4078.

Glistening Waters $$

Glistening Waters and Marina, ☎: 954-3427

Jamaica Room $$

Jamaican, Trelawny Beach Hotel, ☎: 954-2450

Palm Terrace $-$$

Jamaican-Continental, Trelawny Beach Hotel, ☎: 954-2450

tennis courts, riding stables and trails, and bird sanctuary. The 2,000-acre (800 hectare) grounds have a number of historic buildings and contain a water wheel and plantation equipment. Formerly a sugar plantation, the main crops are now papaya, ackee, citrus and anthuriums.

Visit **Luminous Lagoon** at Oyster Bay, just east of Falmouth, which gets its name because of the high concentration of bio-luminous micro-organisms in the water which glow at night when disturbed by a swimmer or a boat. There are nightly guided tours with Glistening Waters, ☎: 954-3229.

From Falmouth you can also take either the Good Hope or Perth Town roads inland to visit the Windsor Caves, which are easily accessible and huge. The coast road runs past Trelawny Beach, White Bay, Coral Spring and Silver Sand to Duncans, where you can take inland road B10 to Clark's Town on the eastern edge of Cockpit Country. This section of coastal road is known as the Queen's Highway and as you drive along you will notice tall metal posts driven into the verges on either side of the road. These were erected to deter light aircraft from landing on the road to pick up drugs. The planes could land on the road, pick up their illegal cargo and take off in a few minutes. Approaching traffic would be held up by men pretending there had been an accident ahead. If any plane attempted to land, the metal posts would rip off its wings.

COCKPIT COUNTRY

This is a fascinating area not just because of its strange geological formations but also because of its rich and proud history. The landscape was carved by water erosion eating into the soft limestone, a process known as karstification. Over a million years or so, water carved out this weird landscape. Harder areas of rock stand out as pinnacles, and the whole region is a mass of caves, natural tunnels, gullies, crags, hillocks and pits covering the southern half of Trelawny parish, an area of more than 500 sq miles (806 sq km). It is the pitted nature of the area that gives it its name and the dense forest cover made it the ideal refuge for the Maroons, the runaway slaves who defied all attempts by the British to capture them, and eventually achieved a sort of self-rule status.

The Maroons were the former slaves of Spanish estate owners who fled when Britain invaded in 1655. The Spanish fled to Cuba and their slaves took to the densely forested mountains to avoid being enslaved by the British. It is not known where the name Maroon came from, but the most likely explanation is that it was either from the French word 'marron' for a runaway slave, or from the Spanish 'cimarran', which meant 'wild'.

There were two major Maroon communities, one based in the Blue Mountains, the Windward Maroons led by Quao and national heroine Nanny, and the other in the near-impenetrable Cockpit Country, the Leeward Maroons led by Kudjoe. The Maroons proved amazingly versatile at surviving in this harsh environment. They tilled gardens in the soils in the base of the pits, some of which were vast. Their numbers grew as other runaway slaves joined them, and all the time they fought a running guerilla war against the

Above and Inset: Columbus Park, Jamaica's only open-air museum

Right: Dunn's Falls

Opposte page above and below: Discovery Bay

Opposte page background: Discovery Bay

British and the plantation owners. Repeated attempts to capture them failed, and in 1738 the British sued for peace. Under the terms of the peace agreement signed on 1 March 1739, they were granted 2,500 acres (1000 hectares) of land and given self-rule of their territories.

In a classic case of poacher turned gamekeeper, the Maroons were then employed by the authorities to track down escaped slaves, and they helped put down the uprising led by Tacky in 1760. The peace was relatively short lived, however, and fighting broke out between the Maroons and the British after the authorities breached the treaty agreement. Vastly outnumbered by a huge and heavily-armed British force, the Maroons agreed to surrender on condition they would not be killed or transported. Even then, the British broke their word, and as the Maroons gave themselves up they were herded aboard ships and sent to Halifax in Nova Scotia, and after four years of deprivation in Canada, they were then transported to Sierra Leone in West Africa.

Little remains of the Maroon presence but the **Maroon Town Barracks** survives at Flagstaff just to the east of Maroon Town in the heart of Cockpit Country, and you can visit their main settlement at **Accompong**, named after Kudjoe's brother. The Maroons still have their own council and elect their own 'Colonel' as leader. The Accompong Maroon Festival is held every January.

Our tour continues by taking the coastal road to the small historic port and fishing town of **Rio Bueno** that is worth exploring. It has a number of old buildings and warehouses, fine old churches and Fort Dundas, built in 1778, to protect the once thriving port. Scenes from the film 'A High Wind in Jamaica' were filmed here. The picturesque Anglican Church was built in 1883 and the Baptist Church in 1901. You can visit the **Arawak Caves** with their rock carvings and artifacts, and the gallery and workshop of Joe James, an internationally acclaimed artist and woodcarver. His extensive studios and gallery are part of the Hotel Rio Bueno, next to the Anglican church.

Continue past the Rio Bueno Travel Halt, a rest stop, to Bengal Bridge, first built in 1798, over the Rio Bueno, which is the boundary between Trelawny parish in Cornwall, and St Ann's in Middlesex. The road then runs to Columbus Park and **Discovery Bay**.

Mystery

The area was originally named Puerto Seco (dry harbor), but was changed to commemorate the landing of Columbus. Actually where he landed is still hotly disputed by historians, and some insist he first came ashore at Rio Bueno, the next river inlet to the west.

The area has prospered because of the bauxite quarry inland run by Kaiser Jamaica, although Discovery Bay is still a small quiet town. Just to the west of town is a marine coral research center run by the University of the West Indies.

Columbus Park is Jamaica's only open-air museum located on a bluff overlooking the Bay marking the spot where Columbus first landed. The museum displays cannon, old agricultural equipment and relics of Jamaica's past. It is open daily.

From Discovery Bay you can take the inland road to connect with the B3 that goes to Brown's Town that is worth a short detour. At **Orange Valley**, you can visit the privately owned 2,300-acre (920 hectare) estate with its large and unusual 'H' shaped Great House. You can see the old stone slave hospital and the eighteenth-century sugar mill and equipment, which was in use until the Second World War. Tours can be arranged through the estate office. There were and still are many large estate in this area, including the **Minard Estate** with two great houses – New Hope and Minard.

Brown's Town became a busy market town because it developed at the intersection of several important roads. Founded by Irishman Hamilton Brown, it is now a delightful, unspoiled hill town, with a traditional market held every Saturday.

RUNAWAY BAY

If you continue south on the B3 and then take the road to Nine Mile from Alexandria, you can visit the birthplace and mausoleum of Rastafarian reggae superstar Bob Marley. His tomb is in a small chapel on top of the hill, and is regarded by many as a shrine, constantly visited and covered in flowers. Every February on his birthday, all-night memorial concerts are held.

Back at the coast, the road runs past the Runaway Caves to **Runaway Bay**. There are two theories as to how the bay got its name. One is that it was where slaves escaping from the plantations would make for and then try to flee the Island in canoes. The other explanation is that it was named by the English because it was where the Spanish Governor fled the Island for Cuba when the English invaded in 1655. Both slaves and the Governor are said to have hidden in the

EATING OUT
• IN AND AROUND RUNAWAY BAY •

The following symbols are used: $ inexpensive, $$ moderate, $$$ expensive.

Great House Dining Room $$-$$$
Jamaican,
☎: 973-2436

Lobster Bowl $-$$
Jamaican-International, Hotel Rio Bueno, ☎: 954-0046

Renaissance Restaurant $$-$$$
French, Ambiance Jamaica Hotel
☎: 973-4705

Sea Shanty Restaurant $$
seafood, Portside Villas ☎: 973-2007

Seaview Restaurant $$
Jamaican-Continental, Club Caribbean ☎: 973-3507

caves during the day. Today the caves offer welcome shade for the tourists who descend on to the beaches, and the cave network runs for about 10 miles (16km). The main feature of the caves, which can be visited by boat, is the **Green Grotto**, 150ft (46m) below ground. Nearby, you can tour the Circle B Farm that still produces fruits and has the ruins of Jamaica's first sugar factory. Dover Raceway, south of Runaway Bay, has both car and motorcycle racing, sometimes with international drivers.

Outside Runaway Bay there is the **Columbus Monument** and the Seville Estate, the site of Sevilla La Nueva, the first Spanish settlement on Jamaica. There is an ongoing program of archaeological excavations to unearth the island's past. **Seville Great House and Heritage Park**, seven miles (11km) west of Ocho Rios, traces the inhabitants of the island back more than 1,500 years to the Tainos, the first Arawak-speaking Amerindians, who called the area Maima. Artifacts from this earliest era are displayed at the Great House. The Park also contains the site of the Spanish Church of Peter Martyr, the ruins of a Spanish fortified castle and the base of a very early Spanish sugar mill. The English named the estate Seville. You can tour the Great House built around 1745 and explore the ruins of the aqueduct and water powered sugar mill, stone wharf, and an African slave settlement area.

SALEM TO OCHO RIOS

The road continues east through **Salem**, where there are eateries, to Chukka Cove where there is Chukka Cove Farm with the most complete

Carvings at the Craft Market, Ocho Rios

Harmony Hall, Ocho Rios

National Hero

M arcus Garvey is credited with much of the ideology behind Rastafarianism, with his rallying cry of: 'One God, One Aim, One Destiny'. His aim was to lead his people back to their birthright in Africa, and in 1914 he founded the Universal Negro Improvement Association (UNIA). Based in Kingston, it sought to create a worldwide coalition of black people who would sustain the economic, cultural and spiritual rebirth of Africa.

In order to gain a wider audience, he moved to the United States where he launched the Negro World newspaper. It had immediate appeal among its target audience and was soon being sold in 40 countries worldwide, although its ideas made him unpopular with many governments and multi-national companies who saw their interests threatened. In 1922 he was charged with mail fraud – he was almost certainly framed – and was sent to prison, but released early in 1924 and deported to Jamaica.

In 1927 he made a speech in Kingston in which he said a black king would be elected in Africa. The king was Haile Selassie of Ethiopia, who became the Black Messiah of Rastafarians. Many Jamaicans, severely hit by the Depression, quickly adopted the new religion. Garvey continued to promote the UNIA and moved its headquarters to London in 1935, where he died five years later. He never managed to visit Africa.

equestrian facility in the Caribbean. Continue to Priory and you can make a small detour inland to the **Circle 'B' Plantation**, where there are walking tours through this small working plantation. Lunch is available.

St Anns is the main town of St Anns parish, and its main claim to fame is as the birthplace of national hero Marcus Garvey. You can also visit the courthouse built in 1860, and the 1750 stone fort, one of the many built along the north coast to protect the harbors from attacks by pirates. The fort was built from stones from the ruins of Sevilla La Nueva.

A small detour from St Anns takes you south through Higgin Town and Claremont to **Pedro**, where you can visit the ruins of **Edinburgh Castle**. This small home was unusual because of its circular towers, and was the home of Lewis Hutchinson, the infamous eighteenth-century mass murderer, known as 'the mad doctor'. He 'befriended' travellers by offering them accommodation, and robbed and killed at least 40 people, mostly by shooting and then beheading! He was captured while trying to flee by ship after killing a neighbor, and hanged in Spanish Town in 1773. In his will he left £100 for the construction of a memorial. The memorial was not built but it is not known what happened to the money – a sizeable sum at the time.

From Pedro you can also drive eastwards to Moneague and then south a short distance to **Schwallenburgh**, where there is a wonderful orchid sanctuary (there is a smaller sanctuary at Martin's Hill in Manchester). At Schwallenburgh there are about 15,000 plants representing about 60 species.

Dunn's River Falls and Park, between **St Anns Bay** and Ocho Rios, is worth visiting for the unique chance to try your hand at waterfall climbing. The wide falls, surrounded by lush vegetation, cascade more than 600ft (183m) in gently sloping terraces that can be scaled. Guides will help you make the slippery ascent, and point out the best route, in return for a tip. There are even night tours of the falls that you climb after dinner. The waters then flow into the Caribbean, and it was in this area that the battle of Los Chorreros was fought, when a Spanish expeditionary force from Cuba was beaten by the English. You can swim in the waters and there is a snack bar and toilets. The park is open from 8am to 5pm daily ☎: 974-2857. There is a second, less visited, waterfall about one mile west on the Roaring River.

OCHO RIOS

Ocho Rios is the second major tourist town on the north coast with a wide range of accommodation, excellent beaches, airstrip and modern cruise facilities. Each year it attracts more than 700,000 tourists, about 350,000 of these from cruise ships, and a major initiative is under to way to upgrade visitor facilities with information booths, toilets, more signs and guides, and a promenade from Reynolds Pier to Dunns River. There has been a crack down on hustlers and illegal vendors, and residents and businesses are being encouraged to plant flowers and trees and properly maintain properties.

The town makes a great base for exploring both the coast and the lush interior with its fast flowing rivers and the many waterfalls, working plantations and beautiful tropical gardens. The combination of sunshine and rainfall are ideal for flowering plants, and the area is usually a blaze of bright hibiscus and poinsettia. If you don't want to spend all your time on the beach or in the water, you can go Calypso rafting or hiking.

Mistaken Name

Ocho Rios is unlike most other north coast towns that used to be busy little ports and are now small fishing villages. What was once a quiet fishing village is now a popular tourist centre and busy port, with bauxite shipments accounting for much of the traffic. Ocho Rios was named after a battle when a Spanish expeditionary force from Cuba was repelled by the English. The Spanish called the area 'chorreros' (Spanish for waterfall) because of the large number of waterfalls in the area, but the English misinterpreted this as ocho rios, meaning eight rivers, and this is the name that stuck. Many of the area's waterfalls have now been tapped to supply hydroelectric power to the resorts.

The tourist development stems from the 1960s when the harbor was dredged and the white sand beach reclaimed. The remains of the fort are just to the west of town, near the bauxite terminal, and were built in the late seventeenth-century.

The town has a bustling market and a range of eating places, and the most popular attractions include the **Carinosa Tropical Gardens, Shaw Park Gardens** which offer stunning views over the town and out to sea, and **Fern Gully** which runs south of town. A new by-pass now diverts most traffic around the town making it much easier to stroll around.

Carinosa is just south of town, set in a beautiful river gorge that runs through tropical rainforest. It has waterfalls, hanging garden, garden walks, aquarium and lakes, and is noted for its huge collection of orchids and ferns.

Places to Visit

Ocho Rios Galleries

The Art Mark
58 Ocean Village, ☎: 974-2243

Bibi's Collectibles
Ocean Village Shopping Centre, ☎: 974-5155

Four Corners Gallery
121 Main St, ☎: 929-2846

Frame Centre Gallery
9 Island Plaza, ☎: 914-2374

Gallery Joe James
Rio Bueno, ☎: 954-0046

Treasure Chest
Taj Mahal Shopping Centre, ☎: 974-2769

•AROUND OCHO RIOS•

The following symbols are used:
$ inexpensive, $$ moderate,
$$$ expensive.

L'Allegro $-$$
Italian, Jamaica Grande, ☎: 974-2201

Almond Tree $$
Jamaican-Continental, pop into the bar and discover why it is always swinging, Hibiscus Lodge Resort, ☎: 974-2333

Blue Cantina $$
Mexican, Main Street, ☎: 927-1700

Bougainvillea Terrace $$-$$$
Jamaican-Continental, Plantation Inn, ☎: 974-5601

Cafe Jamaique $-$$
Jamaican-fast food, Jamaica Grande, ☎: 974-2201

Cutlass Bay Palm Terrace $-$$
Jamaican-American-Continental, Shaw Park Beach Hotel, ☎: 974-2552

Double V $-$$
Best jerk in the area, Main Street, ☎: 974-5998

Dragons $-$$
Chinese Jamaica Grande, ☎: 974-2201

Harmony Hall $$-$$
Jamaican, Harmony Hall Gallery, ☎: 975-4478

Jamaica Inn $$-$$$
Gourmet dining, reservations, Main Street, ☎: 974-2514

Little Pub $-$$
Jamaican-Seafood, Little Bay, ☎: 974-2324

Lobster Pot $$
Seafood, Main Street, ☎: 974-1461

Mallards Court $$
Nightly theme parties with entertainment, Jamaica Grande, ☎: 974-2201

Minnie's $-$$
Vegetarian and seafood, on the beach at Carib, ☎: 974-0236

Ocho Rios Jerk Center $-$$
Jamaican, Main Street, ☎: 974-2549

Parkway $$
Jamaican, Park-Way Inn, ☎: 974-2667

Passage to India $$
Indian, Main Street, ☎: 795-3182

The Restaurant $$-$$$
Gourmet dining, Harmony Hall, ☎: 975-4478

Ruins $$
Chinese, Dacosta Drive, ☎: 974-2789

Sandcastle's Restaurant $$
Jamaican-Continental, Sandcastle's, ☎: 974-2255

Sea Palm $$
Jamaican-International, Golden Seas Beach Resort, ☎: 975-3540

Upton House on the Green $$-$$$
International-Jamaican, Sandal's Golf and Country Club, ☎: 975-0122

Veranda Café $-$$
Continental, Comfort Suites, ☎: 974-8050

There is good shopping in town and at **Ocean Village**, and there is a Craft Park and Old Market Craft Shoppes. The post office is on Main Street, and the tourist office is in the Ocean Village Shopping Centre.

From Ocho Rios continue along the coast through Frankfort to **Harmony Hall**. It is about 4 miles (6km) east of town and was built in the mid-nineteenth century as a Methodist manse next to a pimento estate. Today it is a showcase for many of the island's most talented artists and craftsmen and very well presented. There is an art gallery, craft center, bookshop and boutique and restaurant. It is open from 10am to 6pm daily. ☎: 974-4478

Continue through Caribbean Park and Jamaica Beach to **Rio Nuevo**, the site of a battle where the Spanish defeated the English. The battle site is open daily from 9am to 4pm. The road then goes through Salt Gut and Boscobel Beach to Oracabessa and the very popular **James Bond Beach**, where you can often listen to live reggae performances. See how many Bond film titles you can spot. For instance, the ticket booth is called Money penny and the Changing Rooms bear the sign 'For Your Eyes Only'.

A little further on you pass **Firefly**, the former home of Noel

Coward and now preserved as he left it, thanks to a $250,000 restoration program. It was named after the luminous fireflies seen after dark. The late playwright discovered the site in 1948 while holidaying on the island and staying with Ian Fleming nearby. He bought the 5-acre (2-hectare) hilltop plateau and built the house in 1956 as a retreat. Many of the world's greatest film stars and members of the Royal family were entertained here and he loved it so much he chose to be buried in the grounds.

The spot where the property is located was originally known as Look-Out and had been used by the buccaneer Sir Henry Morgan 300 years earlier to keep watch for pirates. The studio where Noel Coward worked has magnificent views, and he called it 'the room with a view'. Just outside is a marvelous statue of Noel Coward sitting on a bench and looking out to sea. The tour includes a 20-minute biographical video and a walk through the house and grounds. There is an admission fee. The house is preserved as he left it and is now a museum on the life and lifestyle of Noel Coward. There is a small restaurant offering light lunches and afternoon tea. The house and grounds are open from 8.30am to 5.30pm Monday to Saturday ☎: 997-7201. Further down the road is **Goldeneye**, the home of Ian Fleming, the creator of James Bond, but it is not open to the public.

Sprawling **Port Maria** is the capital of St Mary's parish. There is a monument to slave leader Tacky who led an unsuccessful uprising in 1760. The revolt started on the Frontier estate that is at the eastern end of the bay. On the outskirts of town are the ruins of Fort Haldane.

BACK TO KINGSTON

The road then runs inland to Whitehall. Here, you can continue on the A3 to return to Kingston on the route described as part of the eastern tour. Alternatively you can take the B2 to Richmond, Cuffy Gull and Bog Walk and then either take the A1 to Spanish Town and Kingston, or cut through the mountains on the secondary road via Jackson, Sligoville and Swain Springs for Kingston. This route passes a number of peaks, including Copper's Hill 2419feet (739m).

If you cut across to Bog Walk you can head north on the A1 for about 3 miles (5km) to **Linstead**, which is a busy little market town, before returning back to Kingston, via Wakefield and **Hampden Great House**, built in 1779 by Scotsman Archibald Stirling. The house which looks as if it should be somewhere in the Scottish Highlands, is the only Great House on Jamaica with a full two-storied gable wing. The present family, which has owned the house since 1852, escorts you on tours of their home. Of special interest are the magnificent mahogany floors and island mahogany furniture. Mahogany was used not just because it produced some wonderful results, but because it was so hard, it was one of the most resistant timbers to termite attack. The house is set in a 600-acre (240-hectare) sugar estate with working sugar factory. During the harvest that runs from January to July, the factory operates around the clock six days a week. The house is open from 9am to 4pm Monday to Friday ☎: 995-9870.

Ocho Rios

Shaw Park

A tropical garden with waterfalls overlooking the town, and hundreds of species of tropical flowers and birds. It is open from 7.30am to 5.30pm daily.

Fern Gully

A 3-mile (5km) road built along an old riverbed that winds through a lush valley of 30ft (9m) high fern trees. More than 550 native varieties of plants and trees have been recorded here. Open daily

Brimmer Hall

Plantation Estate with its elegant Great House with period furnishings.

Calypso Rafting

Offers a 45-minute bamboo raft ride along the White River through the tropical forests to enjoy the scenery. There is a stop for a swim in the cool mountain river. 9am to 5pm, daily ☎: 974-2527

Ciboney Villa and Spa Resort

man made spa, ☎: 974-1027

Coyaba River Garden and Museum

Next to the Shaw Park Estate, and there are guided tours of the botanical gardens and museum. It is open from 8.30am to 5pm, daily ☎: 947-6235.

Cranbrook Flower Forest

Tropical gardens with river walks and nature trails. ☎: 770-8071. Evening on the White River 7pm to 11pm, Sunday and Tuesday.

Hooves Limited

Horseback riding.
Jamaica Night on The White River, Canoe ride up a torch lit river to the sound of drums. Folklore show, dinner and open bar.

Jolly Roger Cruises

Tironga run day and night cruises from Ocho Rios Harbour aboard an old wooden sailing ship ☎ 974-2323. Murphy Hill is the site of an old working farm in the hills 2000ft (610m) above Ocho Rios, and now a popular sightseeing spot because of the extensive views along the coastline.

Prospect Plantation Tours

West of downtown. The 1,000acre (400 hectare) plantation is thought to have been settled first by the Arawaks. There are daily tours in an open jitney of the working plantation that grows bananas, sugarcane, coconuts and breadfruit. The estate was established by British Member of Parliament Sir Harold Mitchelle. Many of his famous guests planted trees in the ground to commemorate their visit, including Sir Winston Churchill, Pierre Troudeau and Prince Philip. Open: 10.30am, 2pm and 3.30pm, daily ☎: 994-1058.

Puerto Seco Beach

8am to 5pm, daily.
Sans Souci Lido Spa and Resort natural spa, ☎: 974-2353

Seville Great House

Great House and heritage park
Sleepy Hollow Park
Open 10am to 6pm, daily.

Sun Valley Plantation Tour

The 1 1/2 hour tour of this working plantation, tells the history of the property from the slave era to present day. Boxing of bananas for export takes place at the farm. 9am, 1 pm and 2pm, Monday to Friday.

Wassi Art Pottery Works

Great Pond Village, Wilderness Resort Limited: Sport fishing, mini pet zoo, boat ride on pond. 10am to 5pm, daily ☎: 974-5044

3

Accommodation and Sport

ACCOMMODATION

There are more than 150 hotels, inns and guest houses and well over 800 cottages, villas and apartments, which together offer the widest possible range of accommodation to suit all tastes and pockets. There are luxury, all-inclusive resorts, convention hotels and specialist resorts offering diving, golf and tennis. All-inclusive resorts offer excellent value if you want to stay put, but if you want to get out and explore a lot, look for accommodation offering room and breakfast, so that you can eat out at the many excellent island restaurants. There are many campgrounds and budget accommodation can be found in guesthouses, not all of them registered, and in private homes.

Above: Enjoying a game of volley ball on the beach at Montego Bay

• JAMAICA •

KINGSTON AND AREA

Altamont Court Hotel

Altamont Terrace, 56 rooms, $ restaurant, pool, ☎ 929-4497

Christar Villas

Kingston 10 rooms, $$ pool ☎ 978-3933

Courtleigh

Trafalgar Road, 126 rooms, $-$$ restaurant, bar, pub, business center, pools, fitness center ☎ 929-9000

Crowne Plaza

Kingston, 133 rooms, 3 restaurants, bar, fitness center, tennis, conference facilities, ☎ 925-7674

Four Seasons

Ruthven Road, 76 rooms, $$ restaurant, bar, pool ☎ 926-0682

Hilton Kingston

315 rooms $$$ 2 restaurants, 3 bars, pool, tennis, conference facilities, ☎ 926-5430

Island Club Beverly Hills

22 rooms, $$-$$$ restaurants, pool ☎ 978-3914

Le Meridian Jamaica Pegasus

Knutsford Boulevard, 350 rooms, $$-$$$ 2 restaurants, 2 bars, pool, tennis and meeting rooms, ☎ 926-3690

Mayfair

West King's House Circle, 32 rooms, $-$$ restaurant, bar, kitchenettes, pool ☎ 926-1610

Morgan's Harbour

Port Royal, 45 rooms, $$-$$$ dining, pool, beach, watersports, deep sea fishing, ☎ 967-8030

Strawberry Hill

Irish Town in the Blue Mountain foothills, 12 villas, $$$ restaurant, pool villas, ☎ 944-8400

Wyndham

Knutsford Boulevard, 300 rooms, $$-$$$ restaurant, pool, tennis, facilities for the disabled , meeting rooms, ☎ 926-5430

MANDEVILLE AREA AND ST ELIZABETH AREA

Ashton Great House

Luana, Black River, 18 rooms, $$-$$$ restaurant, pool, beach ☎ 965-2036

Astra Country Inn

Ward Avenue, 22 rooms, $$ restaurant, kitchenette, pool ☎ 962-3725

Golf View Apartments

51 rooms, restaurant, bar, pool, mini sports center, ☎ 962-4471

Invercauld Great House and Hotel

Black River, 48 rooms, $$ restaurant, nightly entertainment, pool, tennis, cycling, watersports and meeting facilities ☎ 965-2750

Olde Wharf Hotel

Treasure Beach, 45 rooms, $$ restaurant, pool, tennis ☎ 965-0003

South Sea View Guesthouse

Whitehouse, 8 rooms, $-$$ restaurant, pool, beach ☎ 963-5069

Treasure Beach

Black River, 36 rooms, $$ 2 restaurants, bar, beach, pool and watersports ☎ 965-0110

Villa Bella

Christiana, Manchester, 18 rooms, $
2 restaurants, facilities for the
disabled ☎ 964-2243

MONTEGO BAY AREA

Atrium at Ironshore

33 apartments, $$ restaurant, pool
☎ 953-2605

Belvedere Beach

Gloucester Avenue, 27 rooms, $
restaurant, kitchenettes, pool
☎ 952-0593

Breezes Montego Bay Resort (Superclubs),

124 rooms, $$-$$$ 2 restaurants, 3
bars, pool, beach, watersports
☎ 940-1150

Coral Cliff

Gloucester Avenue, 30 rooms, $
restaurant, bar, gaming rooms, pool
☎ 952-4130

Coyaba Beach Resort

Mahoe Bay, Little River, 50 rooms,
$$-$$$ 2 restaurants, 3 bars, pool,
beach, watersports, tennis, golf and
meeting facilities ☎ 953-9150

Doctors Cave Beach

Gloucester Avenue, 90 rooms and
apartments $$ restaurants,
kitchenettes and pool ☎ 952-4355

Gloucestershire

Gloucester Avenue, 88 rooms,
$-$$ restaurant and pool ☎ 952-4420

Good Hope Great House

10 rooms, restaurant, pool, tennis
☎ 954-3289

Grand Lido Braco (Superclubs)

Rio Bueno, AI, 186 rooms and suites,
4 restaurants, bars, pool, tennis,
9-hole golf course, ☎ 954-000

Half Moon Golf

Tennis and Beach Club, Rose Hall, 419
rooms and suites (some with butler
service), $$-$$$ restaurants, kitchen-
ettes, pool, beach, water-sports, golf,
tennis, horse riding, shopping mall,
theater, medical center and meeting
facilities ☎ 953-2211

Holiday Inn

Rose Hall, 536 rooms, $$-$$$ 3
restaurants, pool, beach, tennis,
watersports and meeting facilities
☎ 953-2486

Holiday Inn Sunspree Resort

523 rooms, $$-$$$ restaurants, 4
bars, pool, beach, tennis, watersports
☎ 953-2486

Hotel Montego

Federal Avenue, 35 rooms,
$ restaurant, bar, kitchenettes and
pool ☎ 952-3287

Jack Tar Village

Gloucester Avenue, 131 rooms,
$$-$$$ restaurants, kitchenettes,
pool, beach and watersports
☎ 952-4340

Jamaica Grandiosa Resort

Ramparts Close, 40 rooms,
$ 2 restaurants, bar and pool
☎ 979-3205

La Mirage

Queen's Drive, 21 rooms, $ restau-
rant and pool ☎ 952-4637

Lifestyles Resort
Gloucester Avenue, 100 rooms, $$
☎ 952-4703

Mango Walk Villas
Mango Walk Road, luxury villas,
$$ restaurant, pool and beach
☎ 952-1472

Montego Bay Club
Gloucester Avenue, 42 rooms,
$$ restaurant, bar, kitchenettes, pool
and 7 tennis courts, ☎ 952-4310

Montego Bay Racquet Club
Sewell Avenue, 25 rooms and 16
villas, $ restaurants, kitchenettes,
pool and tennis ☎ 952-0200

Ritz Carlton Rose Hall
430 rooms $$$, 5 restaurants, bars,
pool, beach, White Witch golf
course, spa, fitness center, ballroom,
tennis, ☎ 953-3534

Royal Court Hotel and Natural Health Retreat
Sewell Avenue, 23 rooms, $$-$$$
restaurants, kitchenettes, pool, gym
and body shop ☎ 952-4531

Sandals Inn, Kent Avenue
52 rooms, All-Inclusive $$-$$$ 2
restaurant, 2 bars, pool, fitness
center and tennis ☎ 952-4140

Sandals Montego Bay
Kent Avenue, 244 rooms,
All-Inclusive $$$ 4 restaurants,
4 bars, fitness center, entertainment,
car rental, tours, departure lounge,
pool, beach, watersports, tennis and
meeting facilities ☎ 952-5510

Sandals Royal Caribbean
Mahoe Bay, 190 luxury rooms, All-
Inclusive $$$ 5 restaurants, bars,
disco, pool, beach, watersports, tennis,
fitness center, nightly entertainment,
private offshore island and meeting
facilities ☎ 953-2231

Winged Victory
Queen's Drive, 16 rooms and suites,
$-$$ restaurant, pool ☎ 952-3891

Wyndham Rose Hall
Rose Hall, 315 rooms,
$$-$$$ 5 restaurants and bars,
pool, beach, watersports, golf, tennis
and meeting facilities ☎ 953-2650

NEGRIL AREA

Bar B Barn Hotel
Norman Manley Boulevard, 24
rooms, $$$ restaurants beach
☎ 957-4267

Beachcomber Club
Norman Manley Boulevard, 46
rooms, $$ restaurant, kitchenettes,
pool and beach ☎ 957-4171

Beaches Inn
$$$ 130 beachside rooms and suites,
3 restaurants, beach grill, 2 pools,
watersports, tennis, meeting rooms,
Sega Center, kids camp,
☎ 957-5100

Beaches Negril
All Inclusive family resort $$$, 225
rooms and suites, 4 restaurants, 7
bars, 3 pools including swim up soda
fountain, fitness center, video games
room, movie theater, arts and crafts
room, nursery and baby sitting
services, beauty salon, entertainment, tennis, watersports,
☎ 957-9270

Couples Negril

All Inclusive 234 rooms and suites, $$$, 3 restaurants, 5 bars, pools, beach, watersports, spa, fitness center, games room, ☎ 957-5960

Grand Lido Superclubs

Norman Manley Boulevard, 200 rooms, Luxury All-Inclusive $$$ 3 restaurants, 9 bars, pool, beach, watersports, tennis and meeting facilities ☎ 957-5010

Heart Beat Guesthouse

West End, 6 rooms, $ restaurant and kitchenettes ☎ 957-4329

Hedonism 11

Norman Manley Boulevard, 280 rooms, Luxury All-Inclusive adults only $$$ 2 restaurants, bar, disco, pool, beach, watersports and tennis ☎ 957-5200

Hog Heaven Hotel

Lighthouse Road, 13 rooms $$, dining room ☎ 957-4991

Mahogany Inn Beach

Norman Manley Boulevard, 16 rooms, $$ restaurant, beach and watersports ☎ 957-4401

Mariner's Inn and Diving Resort

West End, 52 rooms, $$ restaurant, kitchenettes, pool, dive shop, boutique and tennis, ☎ 957-0392

Sandals Negril

Norman Manley Boulevard, 223 rooms and suites, some with butler service, luxury All-Inclusive $$$ restaurants, pool, beach, watersports, tennis, fitness center, full service spa, entertainment and meeting facilities ☎ 957-5216

OCHO RIOS AREA

Boscobel Beach (Superclubs)

207 rooms, All-Inclusive family resort, 3 restaurants, 5 bars, pool, beach, watersports and tennis ☎ 975-7330

Breezes Golf and Beach Resort

Casa Maria, Port Maria, 20 rooms, $-$$ 2 restaurants, bar, kitchenette, pool and private beach ☎ 994-2323

Ciboney

300 rooms, All-Inclusive villa property $$$ 6 restaurants, 7 bars, kitchenettes, pool, private beach club, watersports and tennis ☎ 974-1027

Club Jamaica

95 rooms, $$-$$$ restaurant, bar-nightclub, pool, beach and watersports ☎ 974-6632

Comfort Suites

Crane Ridge, 75 rooms $$-$$$, restaurant, kitchen facilities, pool, tennis ☎ 974-8050

Couples

St Ann, 175 rooms, All-Inclusive $$$ 4 restaurants and bars, pool, beach, watersports, tennis ☎ 975-4271

Portside Resort and Villas

Discovery Bay, 35 rooms $$, restaurant, bar, pool and watersports, ☎ 973-2007

Renaissance Jamaica Grande

St Ann, 720 rooms, $$$ 5 restaurants, 8 bars, 3 pools, disco, casino, fitness center, children's programs, beach, watersports, tennis and meeting facilities ☎ 974-2200

**Above and Right:
Sandals resort,
Montego Bay**

**Below: Hedonism II,
Montego Bay**

Sandal's Dunn's River Golf Resort and Spa

St Ann, 256 rooms, All-Inclusive $$$
4 restaurants, 7 bars, pools, beach,
watersports, tennis, golf, fitness
center, full service European spa, car
rental, tours and meeting facilities,
☎ 972-0563

Sandal's Ocho Rios Resort and Golf Club

237 rooms, All-Inclusive $$$ 4
restaurants, bars, pools, watersports,
tennis, golf, fitness center, entertainment and meeting facilities
☎ 974-5691

San Souci Lido Ocho Rios (Superclubs)

All Inclusive, 146 rooms, 3 restaurants, bars, pools, spa, ☎ 994-1206

Sea Palms

44 rooms $$, kitchenettes, pool,
beach ☎ 974-4400

Village Hotel

Main Street, 60 rooms, $$ restaurant, disco, health bar and kitchen-
ettes ☎ 974-9193

PORT ANTONIO AREA

Bonnie View Plantation

20 rooms, $$-$$$ restaurant and
pool ☎ 993-2752

Crystal Springs Resort

12 rooms $$ restaurant and pool,
☎ 996-1400

Dragon Bay Beach Resort

90 rooms and 30 villas, $$-$$$
restaurants, beach, scuba, tennis and
watersports ☎ 993-8751

Fern Hill Club

San San, 31 rooms, $-$$ restaurant,
bar, kitchenette, pool and tennis
☎ 993-7374

Goblin Hill

44 rooms, $$-$$$ restaurant,
kitchenette or personal cook, pool
and tennis ☎ 925-8108

Jamaica Crest Villas

14 rooms $$ restaurant, kitchen
facilities, pool ☎ 993-8400

Mocking Bird Hill

Eco-tourism resort, 10 rooms, $$
Mille Fleurs Restaurant and beach
☎ 993-7134

Navy Island Marina Resorts

13 rooms, $$ restaurants, pool,
beach, tennis and watersports
☎ 993-2667

Trident Villas and Hotel

26 rooms, $$-$$$ restaurant, pool,
beach, tennis and watersports, dive
school, watersports ☎ 993-2602

Triff's Inn

Bridge Street, 15 rooms, $$ restaurant ☎ 993-2162

RUNAWAY BAY AREA

Alamanda Inn

Runaway Bay, 20 apartments $$
☎ 973-4030

Breezes Golf and Beach Resort (Superclubs)

234 rooms $$$, 2 restaurants, 4 bar,
nightclub, pools, golf, tennis,
watersports ☎ 973-2436

Caribbean Isle

23 rooms, $$-$$$ restaurant, pool and beach ☎ 973-2634

Club Ambiance

90 rooms and suites, All-Inclusive $$ restaurant, pool, beach and watersports ☎ 973-2066

Club Caribbean

135 cottages and 20 one-room suites, $$-$$$ restaurant, pool, tennis and watersports ☎ 973-4675

Caribbean Isle

23 rooms $$, restaurant, pool ☎ 973-2364

Club Ambience

82 rooms $$ restaurant, pool, watersports ☎ 973-2066

Eaton Hall Beach

50 rooms, All-Inclusive $$$ restaurant, pool, beach, watersports and tennis ☎ 973-3503

Franklyn D. Resort

67 suites, All-Inclusive $$-$$$ 2 restaurants, 4 bars, kitchenettes, pool, beach, watersports and tennis ☎ 973-4591

Grand Lido Braco

180 rooms $$-$$$ 4 restaurants, bar, pool, beach, golf, watersports ☎ 954-000

Hedonism III

225 room including Jamaica's first swim-up rooms, adults only resort, 4 restaurants, bars, disco, 3 pools (one au natural), two beaches (one au natural), circus workshop, tennis, watersports ☎ 973-5029

Jamaica Jamaica

238 rooms, All-Inclusive $$$ restaurants, pool, beach, watersports, tennis, golf and meeting facilities ☎ 973-2436

Runaway Bay HEART (Hotel and Training Institute) Country Club

20 rooms, $$ restaurant and pool ☎ 973-2671

Tamarind Tree

25 rooms, $$ restaurant and pool ☎ 973-2678

Tropical Inn

13 rooms, $ ☎ 973-4681

VILLAS AND APARTMENTS

The Jamaica Association of Villas and Apartments (JAVA) ☎ 974-2508, offers a choice of more than 300 properties, many with pool or on the beach, and most staffed with a cook, gardener and housekeeper. Negril, Montego Bay, Falmouth and area, Discovery and Runaway Bays, Mammee Bay, Ocho Rios and Port Antonio are the main locations.

ALTERNATIVE CAMPING

Maya Lodge is the headquarters of the Jamaica Alternative Camping and Hiking Association (JATCHA) ☎ 927-2097, and the home base of Sense Adventures in the Blue Mountains. The Lodge is set in 16 acres (6.4 hectares) of fruit trees at 1750ft (534m), surrounded by streams and tropical flora. It has nine rooms and rustic cabins, hostel accommodation for 17 and 15 camping sites. It makes an excellent base from which to explore the Blue Mountains.

SPORTS

Jamaica offers world class diving

For the visitor, there is a huge range of sporting opportunities from swimming and scuba diving, to horseback riding and hiking, to golf and tennis. There is cycling, sailing, squash and, of course, fishing either from shore or boat. Most hotels offer a variety of sports and water activities, and there are diving schools where you can learn what it is all about and progress to advanced level if you have the time.

CRICKET

Cricket is the national game and played with such a fervor that it is not surprising that the West Indies are world champions. The game is played at every opportunity and anywhere, and just as fervently by the women as the men. You can be driving in the countryside, turn a corner and confront players using the road as a wicket. It is played on the beach using a strip of palm for a bat, and even in the water if the tide is coming in. If the island team or the West Indies is playing, almost all the radios on the island are tuned in for the commentary, and matches at Sabina Park always draw huge crowds.

And, when cricket is not being played, football (soccer) is the top sport. Just how much Jamaicans love all sports, is shown by the fact that they even entered a national Bobsled team in the 1988 Winter Olympics! Walking is great fun and there are lots of trails, especially in the mountains but have stout, non-slip footwear and a waterproof. Protect yourself against insects, carry adequate drinking water and keep an eye on the time, because night falls quickly and you don't want to be caught out on the trail after dark. Guides can be arranged to escort you on these walks and make sure you get the most out of your trip.

CYCLING

Bikes are available for rent at a number of resorts and bike rental companies. These include:

Montego Bike Rentals
Montego Bay ☎ 952-4984

Carol's Bike Rental
☎ 957-4207

Elvie's Bike Rental
☎ 957-4331

Negril Bike Rentals
☎ 957-4357

Rhodes Hall Plantation
☎ 957-4232, and

Taurus Bike Rental
☎ 957-4409, all in Negril, and

Motor Trails
☎ 974-5058 in Ocho Rios.

Rusty's X-cellent Adventures
Negril ☎ 957-0155.

DEEP SEA FISHING
There is excellent deep-sea fishing for world-record beating fish. The best fishing is generally found off the north coast where catches include dorado, wahoo, blue and white marlin, yellowfin tuna and sailfish. Most Hotels and resorts offer fishing trips and there are many charter boats available. A party of 4 should expect to pay about US$300 for a half-day all-in charter including boat, crew and tackle. Independent charters include:

MONTEGO BAY

Don One Watersports
☎ 952-9391

Montego Bay Yacht Club
☎ 978-8038

Rhapsody
☎ 979-0104

Seaworld
☎ 953-2188

NEGRIL

Best Boat Reef Tour
☎ 995-9709

Blue Whale Divers
☎ 957-4438

Dolphin Divers
☎ 957-4944

Irie Watersports
☎ 957-4670

Neptune and Wild Thing
☎ 957-4401/4402

Sea Raider and Our Past Time
☎ 957-4224

OCHO RIOS

Broadreach Cruises
☎ 973-3507

King Fisher and Sun Fisher
☎ 974-2260

Mitzy
☎ 974-2527

Sunfisher
☎ 994-2294

Triple 'B'
☎ 975-3273

PORT ANTONIO

Bonita 11
☎ 993-3086

DIVING
The waters off Jamaica offer world-class diving. The waters are clear and warm and teem with marine life. There are dives to suit all levels of experience, ranging from shallow reefs and caverns to trenches, deep walls and drop offs, mostly off the north and west coasts. The furthest dive sites are only a 25-minute ride by dive boat from shore. The waters are warm with year-round temperatures averaging between 80° and 90°F (26° and 32°C), and wet suits are not needed for

warmth. The Jamaica Association of Dive Operators (JADO) and the Negril Coral Reef Preservation Society (NCRPS) work closely to establish marine parks. They also install mooring buoys at the most popular sites so that boats can tie up to them rather than drop anchor and damage the coral reefs. The reefs are host to large numbers of tropical fish and a wide range of marine plants and animals. There are filefish, squirrelfish, grunts, barracudas, stingrays, eels and turtles. Coral formations include barrel, vase, and tube sponges, sea fans, and deep-water gorgonian and black coral.

The main reef sites are:

Negril. The reefs start at the West Coast seven-mile (11km) beach and run south and west out to sea. Most of the dive sites are within a ten to 20 minute boat ride, and dive depths range from 20 to 90ft (6 to 27 meters). Apart from the reef there are tunnels, overhangs, caves and plane wrecks, and marine life includes kingfish, nurse sharks, moray eels and stingrays. Southern dive sites include Whaler's Reef, Shangri-La Drop Off, Grotto Reef, Sand's Club Reef, Hanging Garden, Throne Room, Awee Maway, Rock Cliff Reef and Lighthouse Reef. Dive sites to the west of Negril include Coral Gardens, Shark's Reef and Spade Fish Reef.

Montego Bay. This was the site of Jamaica's first marine sanctuary, and many of the dive sites are close to shore over shallow reefs, although there are some awesome walls. At Basket Reef there is a wall that starts at 50ft (15m) below water and drops vertically to 150ft (45m). It is a good site to see dolphin, black durgons and parrot fish. Dive sites include Airplane Wreck, Frenchman's Hole, King Fish Point, Bloody Bay Reef, Treasure Reef, Ballard's Reef, Gallery, Lower and Upper Arch, Basket Reef, No Name Reef, Pillar Collar Reef, Canyon 1 and 2, Black Coral Rock, the Window, Duppy's Hole and the Arena. Offshore and to the east of Montego Bay are Widowmaker's Cave, Rotal Slope, Tyre Reef, the Pit and Double Wall. Airport Reef and Wall is considered one of the island's best dive sites, with a large number of coral caves, tunnels and canyons.

Falmouth. The famous wall off Falmouth is within half a mile (0.8km) of the shore in about 35ft (11m) of water. Other sites include Chub Castle with its bask sponges and wall with black coral and rope sponges, and chimney which descends to 90ft (27m) and further tunnels and caverns.

Runaway Bay. There are good dive sites in shallow waters just off shore, and a wall that forms part of the Cayman Trench. Dive sites include the Canyon with its two parallel walls 20ft (6m) apart in 40ft (12m) of water, and descending to more than 130ft (40m). Other sites are Ricky's Reef, Silver Spray, High Rock, Airplane Wreck, Peartree Bottom, Shipwreck Reef and Spanish Anchor.

Ocho Rios. Devil's Reef is a pinnacle just offshore which drops from 60ft (18m) to 200ft (61m), with a large sand shelf at 130ft (40m). There are a number of tunnels in the Caverns, a shallow quarter-mile (0.4km) long reef with the wreck of the 140 foot (43m) **Kathryn** close-by. Other sites include Moxon's Reef, Fantasea Flat, Chubb Reef, Rio Nievo, Canyon Reef and Key Hole.

Port Antonio. Sites include Alligator Point and Head, Frenchman's Cove, San San Reef, Blue Lagoon Reef and High Point.

Kingston. There are many good dive sites off Port Royal near Kingston airport. The waters contain many old wrecks and there are legends of sunken treasure.

There are several licensed diving centers offering equipment hire and full training. These include:

Falmouth Caribbean Amusements
Falmouth ☎ 954-3427

Fisherman's Inn Dive Resort
Falmouth ☎ 247-0475

Trelawny Beach Hotel
☎ 954-2450.

MONTEGO BAY

Jamaica Rose Divers
☎ 953-2714

Jamaqua Watersports
☎ 956-7050

Montego Bay Fun Dives
☎ 953-2650

North Coast Marine
☎ 953-2211

Poseidon Divers
☎ 952-5909

Reef Keepers
☎ 979-0102

Resort Dives
☎ 973-5750

Sandals Divers
☎ 952-5510

Seaworld Resorts
☎ 953-2550/2486

Scuba Connection
☎ 952-4780

Wyndham Rose Hall
☎ 953-2650

NEGRIL

Blue Whale Divers
☎ 957-4436

Couples
☎ 957-5960

Hedonism II
☎ 957-4200

Negril Scuba Centre
☎ 957-4425/4370

Resort Divers
☎ 957-4061/4010

Sun Divers Negril
☎ 957-4069

Village Resorts
☎ 957-4200

West Point Watersports
☎ 957-9170

Mariners Inn
☎ 957-4384

Sea Horse
☎ 957-4478

Dolphin Divers
☎ 957-4944

RUNAWAY BAY/ OCHO RIOS

Breezes
☎ 973-2436

Couples
☎ 975-4271

Enchanted Gardens
☎ 972-1937

Fantasea Divers
☎ 974-2552

Garfields Dive Station
☎ 974-5749

Island Dive Shop
☎ 972-2519

Jamaica Fun Cruises
☎ 972-2117

Sea and Dive Jamaica
☎ 974-5762

Two views of the coral reef with its marine life

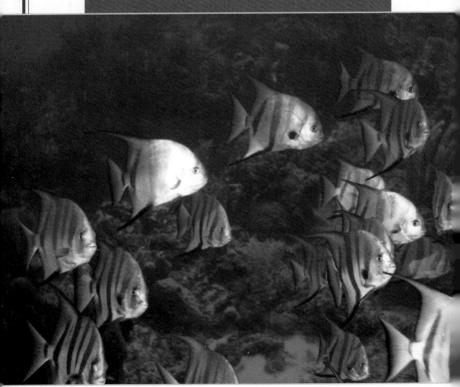

Sundivers Runaway Bay
☎ 973-2006/2345

PORT ANTONIO

Lady G Diver
☎ 993-9888

KINGSTON

Kingston Buccaneer Scuba Club
☎ 967-8061

GOLF

Golf has been played on the island for almost 100 years and there are 12 courses (11 18-hole and one nine-hole) to choose from. The Johnnie Walker World Championship, which brings together 28 of the world's top players, is hosted at Tryall's Golf, Tennis and Beach Club each December. The courses are:

Caymanas Golf Club

18 holes par 72, is six miles from Kingston, and was the island's first championship course, built by Howard Watson in the 1950s. It has snack bar, bar and pro shop ☎ 922-3386

Constant Spring

18 holes par 70, was built in the 1920s by Stanley Thompson in one of Kingston's finest residential areas. It has clubhouse, restaurant, bar and pro shop, as well as tennis, squash, badminton and swimming ☎ 924-1610

Manchester Country Club

9 holes par 35, is in Mandeville and more than 2000 ft (610m) above sea level. It was built more than 100 years ago and was the island's first course. It has nine greens and 18 tee boxes that allow it to be played as an 18-hole course. There is a clubhouse, with bar, tennis and billiards ☎ 962-2403

Half Moon Golf Club

8 holes par 72, is in the 400-acre (160 hectares) Half Moon Resort near Montego Bay, and was designed by Robert Trent Jones. There is clubhouse, restaurant, bar and pro shop, with tennis and squash ☎ 953-3105

Ironshore Golf and Country Club

18 holes par 72, near Montego Bay and designed by Canadian Robert Moote. It has a clubhouse, restaurant, bar and pro shop ☎ 953-2800.

Negril Hills

a new 18 holes par 72 course four miles (6.5km) from Negril, on a resort featuring cottage accommodation and a pro shop ☎ 957-4638

Ritz Carlton Rose Hall

18-hole championship White Witch Course ☎ 953-3534

Sandals Golf and Country Club

18 holes par 71, is 2 miles (3km) from Ocho Rios and 700ft (213m) above sea level, and is one of the island's most beautiful courses. It has clubhouse, bar and pro shop ☎ 975-0119

San San Golf and Country Club

9 holes, has recently been refurbished and is in one of Jamaica's most beautiful areas close to Port Antonio ☎ 993-9345

Breezes Golf and Beach Resort

18 holes par 72, at Runaway Bay, was designed by James D. Harris in the late 1960s. It has a clubhouse, restaurant, pro shop and tennis ☎ 973-2561

Tryall Golf, Tennis and Beach Club

18 holes par 71, is 12 miles from Montego Bay, and was built in 1960 by Texan architect Ralph Plummer on the site of a nineteenth-century sugar plantation. It has clubhouse, beach bar and restaurant, pro shop and tennis ☎ 956-5681

Wyndham Rose Hall Country Club

18 holes par 72, is east of Montego Bay, and home of the Jamaica Open. The course was built in the 1970s by Henry O. Smedley and has clubhouse, restaurant, bar, pro shop and tennis ☎ 953-2650

HORSEBACK RIDING

Riding is available in all resort areas. The Chukka Cove Equestrian Centre, between Ocho Rios and Runaway Bay, is a world class polo and riding facility, with guided rides along the beach and into the mountains ☎ 972-2506

DISCOVERY BAY

Braco Stables
☎ 954-000

MONTEGO BAY AREA

Barnett Estate Great House
☎ 952-2382

Rocky Point Stables
☎ 953-2286.

NEGRIL AREA

Country Western Stables
☎ 957-3250.

SOUTH COAST

Ashton Great House
☎ 965-2036

HORSE RACING AND POLO

There is horse racing at the track at Caymanas Park, or enjoy a game of polo over a cup of tea at Caymanas, Chukka Cove, Drax Hall, Blue Hole, or Hanover.

JOGGING

The resort areas have jogging trails or tracks. There is an annual Run for Fun meet for amateurs each year in November.

SAILING AND SURFING

There is parasailing and windsurfing at Negril, and there is excellent windsurfing along the north coast. You can rent equipment at most oceanfront Hotels and on some public beaches. At Boston Beach the waves are high enough for surfing.

SWIMMING

There are 200 miles (322km) of beaches, and there are public beaches in all resort areas.

TENNIS

Many of the large hotels and resorts have courts, and several offer floodlit tennis. If you are new to the island, book courts for early in the day or late in the afternoon so that you do not play when the sun is at its strongest. The Half Moon Celebrity Tennis Tournament is held each December at the Half Moon Resort in Montego Bay.

WATER SKIING

The Blue Lagoon in Port Antonio and Doctor's Cave Beach in Montego Bay are ideal locations, but so is just about everywhere else. Equipment rental is widely available.

WATERFALL CLIMBING

A rare opportunity to safely scale some of the island's many beautiful falls. Climb the gently terraced stairway at Dunn's River Falls with 600ft (183m) of cascades, or take a dip at Somerset Falls and Reach (Reich) Falls.

GETTING THERE:

By air. There are two international airports – Norman Manley International Airport in Kingston Harbour, and Donald Sangster International Airport at Montego Bay in the northwest corner of the island.

From the US and Canada: There are direct flights on Air Jamaica from Toronto (4 hours), Chicago and Newark (3 hours 45 minutes), Newark, New York (3 hrs 20 min), Baltimore and Washington (3 hrs), Los Angeles (5 hours 30 minutes), Fort Lauderdale (1 hour 35 minutes), Orlando (1 hour 50 minutes), Phoenix, Philadelphia (4 hrs 30 min), Atlanta (2 hrs 40 min) and Miami (1 hr 25 min), on American Airlines from New York and Miami, on NorthWest from Minneapolis and Tampa, on Continental from Newark, on Air Canada from Toronto (4 hrs), Montreal, Halifax and Winnipeg, Canadian Holidays from Toronto, and US Air from Philadelphia and Charlotte. American Trans Air fly from Indianapolis, Fort Lauderdale (winter) and Orlando (summer), and TWA fly from St Louis.

From Europe: There are direct Air Jamaica flights from London and Manchester, British Airways flights from London Gatwick (10hrs 15min), and Thomsons, Britannia Charter, Airtours and UniJet operate charters from Manchester and Gatwick. Condor flies from Frankfurt. American Airlines, British Airways and Virgin fly from London to Miami with connecting flights on Air Jamaica.

Air Jamaica Express, BWIA, Cayman Airlines, Caribbean Airlines and Trans Jamaica operate services between Jamaica and other Caribbean islands. Air Jamaica also flies between Jamaica and Grand Cayman and Nassau in the Bahamas.

Shortly after landing and while you are still strapped in your seat, the crew may come through the cabin spraying insecticide. It is harmless to humans but kills any stowaway bugs which might damage the island's agriculture. On arrival, be sure to enjoy a welcoming glass of rum at the courtesy stand if it is open. ⁻

By Sea: Cruise ships regularly call at Montego Bay, Ocho Rios and Port Antonio. Cruise lines include Carnival Cruise, Celebrity/Fantasy, Commodore, Costa, Crown (Cunard), Dolphin, Holland America, Norwegian, Premier, Princess, Regency, Royal Caribbean and Sun Cruises. Most operate out of Miami, West Palm Beach, Tampa and Fort Lauderdale, all in Florida, and New Orleans.

Ocho Rios, Port Antonio and Negril are also major ports. There are no ferry services between Jamaica and the US or other Caribbean islands.

Airports/Airways

ALM Kingston
☎ 926-1762

Air Canada Kingston
☎ 924-8211
Montego Bay
☎ 952-5160

Air Jamaica Kingston
☎ 888-359-2475, 922-4661
Montego Bay
☎ 952-4100
Negril
☎ 957-4210
Ocho Rios
☎ 974-2566, and in the
US 1-800-523-5585

Air Jamaica Express
☎ 923-8680/888-359-2475

American Airlines Kingston
☎ 920-8887

BWIA Kingston
☎ 888-991-2210

British Airways Kingston
☎ 929-9020
Montego Bay
☎ 952-3771

Caribbean Airlines Kingston
☎ 960-1990
Montego Bay
☎ 952-8611

Caribic Airways
☎ 952-5013

Cayman Airways Kingston
☎ 926-1762

Continental Airlines
Montego Bay
☎ 952-5530

NorthWest Airlines
Montego Bay
☎ 800-225-2525

Timair (air taxi)
☎ 952-2516

US Air
☎ 800-622-1015

BANKS

Banks are open from 9am to 2pm Monday to Friday and 9am to 12noon and 2.30 to 5pm on Friday. They are not open at weekends and on pubic holidays.

BEACHES

The island boasts many spectacular beaches although some areas close to large hotels and resorts may be reserved for guests. The best beaches in the north include: Alterry Beach, Braco, Cardiff Hall, Damali, Puerto Secco Beach in Discovery Bay, Golden Head, Half Moon, Mammee Bay, Montego Bay, especially Doctors Cave, Walter Fletcher Beach and Cornwall Beach, Murdocks, Orange Bay, Rio Bueno, Rose Hall, on Peter's Island off Port Antonio, Roxborough Beach and Turtle Beach. On the east coast beaches include: Boston, Holland Bay, Long Bay and San San. Along the south coast there are: Alligator Pond, Bailey's Beach, Black River, Bluefields, Brooks Pen, Cable Hut, Flemarie, Fort Clarence, Gunboat Beach, Hellshire, Jackson Bay, Lime Cay, Lyssons Providence Pen, Prospect, Retreat, Treasure Beach and Whitehouse. Along the west coast there are the beaches of Negril Bay and Watson Taylor. Note: A few resorts permit nude bathing on designated beaches.

Above: **Relaxing in the pool at the Beaches resort in Negril** *Below:* **Treasure Beach**

BICYCLES, MOPEDS AND SCOOTERS

Bicycles are available for rent at several resorts and there are many cycle rental shops, especially in Negril. Mopeds and scooters are available but must be ridden with extreme caution in view of road conditions and other road users. Rusty's X-cellent Adventures in Negril offers guided cycle tours of the area ☎ 957-0155.

CAR RENTAL

To rent a car you must be at least 21 years old although many companies have a minimum age of 25. You need a valid driver's license and a major credit card. A refundable deposit is required on all rental cars.

A North American driving license is valid for up to 90 days, a UK driver's license is valid for up to 12 months, and a Japanese driving license is valid for up to 30 days.

Car rental costs from US$65 to $120 a day, and US$325 a week. Rates include third party insurance, but not personal accident insurance or damage to the vehicle. There is a government tax of 12.5% on all rentals. Always check the rental car before driving away. Check the conditions of the tires, make sure there is a good spare, and that the brakes are in good working order. Pot holes can cause considerable damage to both tires and brakes.

Cars drive on the left and the speed limit is 30mph (50kph) in towns and 50mph (80kph) on rural highways. Road distances are now generally given in kilometres. Service stations are open daily until about 7pm, but only accept cash for gas. There are rest stops on several of the main highways and these are usually open daily between 9am and 8pm. Between Falmouth and Runaway Bay there are rest stops at Rio Bueno, Traval Halt and Rio Braco, with toilets, light refreshments and the chance to buy local arts and crafts. There is also a rest stop in Bamboo Avenue in St Elizabeth.

If you are involved in an accident, report it to the local police as quickly as possible, and write down the details of other drivers, how the accident happened, who was at fault and the names and addresses of any witnesses, and if possible, get the other parties to sign it.

In the event of a breakdown, contact the car rental company as quickly as possible for a replacement. At night, contact the police who can usually get in touch with the car rental company.

Driving Times:

Kingston to Montego Bay 4 hours

Montego Bay to Negril 1.5 hours

Montego Bay to Ocho Rios 1.5-2 hours

Montego Bay to Port Antonio 4.5-5 hours

Kingston to Port Antonio 2 hours

Kingston to Mandeville 1.5 hours

Fact File

Kingston to Negril	**Kingston to Ocho Rios**
4 hours	1 hour 30 minutes

Car rental companies include:

Avis Rent-a-Car
Montego Bay
☎ 952-5195

Budget Rent-a-Car
Motego Bay
☎ 952-3838

Discovery Transport
Port Antonio
☎ 993-9625

Galaxy Car Rentals
Kingston
☎ 925-4176

Hertz
Montego Bay
☎ 979-0438

Villa Car Rentals
Ocho Rios
☎ 974-2975

Main roads encircle the island and there are three major north south crossings through the mountains. The most spectacular route is the Old Kingston Highway that runs from Kingston to Port Antonio through the Blue Mountains. Road conditions vary enormously, many side roads are badly pot holed, and many roads are not signposted which adds to the adventure and explains why a good road map is essential. Car hire is expensive but advisable if you want to do a lot of exploring, and while mopeds and motor cycles can be rented, they are not advisable for off the beaten track exploration because of some of the road conditions. Drivers sound their horns a lot, especially when approaching blind corners, so be attentive. And, because of the winding and often mountainous nature of the roads, always overestimate how long it will take to get one from one place to another. Journeys almost always take longer than planned because there are so many photo opportunities, tempting beaches and Jamaican fast food roadside stalls. Jamaican drivers also love to stop suddenly and chat to friends by the roadside, and animals frequently stray onto the roads.

CHURCHES

All the main religious denominations are represented. In Kingston there is the Bethel Baptist Church, Bethel United Pentecostal Church, Jewish Synagogue, Kingston Episcopal Parish Church, St Andrew's Episcopal Church, the Roman Catholic Church of Saints Peter and Paul, the Webster Memorial Presbyterian Church and Coke Methodist Church. In Montego Bay there is the Blessed Sacrament Roman Catholic Cathedral, Calvary Baptist Church, Holy Trinity Episcopal Church, Kings Chapel United Pentecostal Church and St James Episcopal Parish Church. At Ocho Rios there is the Church of God Of Prophecy, Methodist Church, Ocho Rios Baptist Church, Our Lady of Fatima Catholic Church, and St Johns Anglican Church. In Port Antonio there are Baptist, Anglican and Methodist Churches, Salvation Army, St Anthony's Catholic Church and Shiloh

Fact File

Apostolic Evangelical Church, and in Negril, there is the St Mary Anglican Church, United Church Jamaica Grand Cayman, and Roman Catholic Church.

CLOTHING AND PACKING

Light, loose and informal clothing is best. Swimwear is fine on the beach or by the pool, but cover up a little if walking around town or going for a meal. Most hotels and restaurants do not have dress codes, although some prefer men to wear jackets but not ties, for dinner. Many people, however, after spending a day on the beach like to dress up for dinner and there are no problems if you want to do this.

Evening temperatures can dip just a little, and a sweater, light jacket or wrap can come in useful. Pack sandals for the beach as the sand can get too hot to walk on, and if you plan to go walking in the interior, take lightweight trousers and sturdy footwear. A lightweight waterproof jacket is also a good idea if you plan to go hiking, sailing or similar.

A hat, sunglasses and a good sunscreen lotion are also essential, and if you don't have a sun hat, buy a straw hat as soon as you arrive on the island because they are perfect for the job and make great souvenirs.

CURRENCY AND CREDIT CARDS

The official currency is the Jamaican dollar (JA$), although US dollars are widely accepted. The JA$ comes in bills of 1,2,5,10, 20, 50 and 100 dollars. The official exchange rate varies and it is best to exchange currency at banks. You will generally get a less favorable exchange rate at exchange bureaus and hotels, and you are likely to be ripped off if you exchange currency on the street. As a rough guide US$1=JA$40 and UK£1= JA$ 60. All major credit cards are accepted. Currencies officially recognized by the Jamaican government may also be used to settle hotel, restaurant or car rental bills and duty free shopping. When exchanging money into Jamaican dollars, do not get more than you need as you are not allowed to take Jamaican currency out of the country. If you have to convert surplus Jamaican dollars back into a foreign currency before leaving, you will have to pay another exchange fee, and remember to keep the foreign exchange receipt for possible inspection on departure.

CUSTOMS AND IMMIGRATION

For stays of less than six months proof of identification and an onward return ticket are required. US and Canadian citizens need either a valid passport, or one that has expired within the last year, or an original or certified copy of birth certificate, naturalization certificate or laminated picture ID, or US or Canadian voter registration card together with a photo driver's license. For Japanese visitors a valid passport is required and a visa if planning a stay of more than 30 days, and for British and Commonwealth citizens, a valid passport is needed with at least six months to run after the date of onward return journey. Visas may be necessary for nationals of other countries.

Visitors arriving in Jamaica are allowed to bring in 200 cigarettes, 25 cigars, one quart of alcohol (except rum), one pound (0.4kg) of tobacco and one quart of wine. The import of flowers, fruit, plants, honey, vegetables, coffee and meat is restricted.

Departing US visitors are allowed to take up to US$600 of purchases, although all items manufactured or produced in Jamaica (coffee, rum, perfume, arts and crafts) are duty free. Canadian visitors are allowed to take back C$500 worth of goods a year. Japanese visitors are allowed to take home up to US$1700 worth of duty free goods.

DEPARTURE TAX

There is a departure tax of JA$1,000 or equivalent in US dollars.

ELECTRICITY

The electrical supply is generally 110 volts/50 cycles although some hotels also provide 220 volts. European appliances will need plug adaptors.

EMERGENCY NUMBERS

Police 119   **Fire/Ambulance** 110   **Air Sea Rescue** 119

GAMBLING

There are no casinos although many resorts feature slot machines such as the Coral Cliff Gaming Park in Montego Bay. There is horse racing at the Caymans Racetrack in Kingston.

HEALTH

There are no serious health problems although visitors should take precautions against the sun and biting insects such as sand flies and mosquitoes, both of which can ruin your holiday. Biting bugs tend to come out late in the afternoon. Other minor problem areas include one or two nasty species of wasps, and there are scorpions although these are very rare, and their sting is usually painful rather than dangerous. Be careful around coral and be alert for jellyfish and spiny sea urchins that are occasionally a problem at some times of the year.

Immunization is not required unless traveling from an infected area, or one of the following areas within the previous six weeks – Asia, Africa, Central and South America, Dominican Republic, Haiti, and Trinidad and Tobago.

Most hotels and resorts have doctors on call around the clock, and emergency dental treatment is also available at all times.

Tanning safely

The sun is very strong but sea breezes often disguise just how hot it is. If you are not used to the sun, take it carefully for the first two or three days, use a good sunscreen with a factor of 15 or higher, and do not sunbathe during the hottest parts of the day. Wear sunglasses and a sun hat. Sunglasses will protect you against the glare, especially strong on the beach, and sun hats will protect your head.

If you spend a lot of time swimming or scuba diving, take extra care, as you will burn even quicker because of the combination of salt water and sun. Calamine lotion and preparations containing aloe are both useful in combating sunburn.

Irritating insects

Mosquitoes can be a problem almost anywhere. In your room, burn mosquito coils or use one of the many electrical plug-in devices that burn an insect repelling tablet. Mosquitoes are not so much of a problem on or near the beaches because of onshore winds, but they may well bite you as you enjoy an open-air evening meal. Use a good insect repellant, especially if you are planning trips inland such as walking in the rain forests. Fire ants are also found in wooded areas, and their bites can be very irritating. Bay rum essences can be soothing.

Lemon grass can be found growing naturally, and a handful of this in your room is also a useful mosquito deterrent.

Sand flies can be a problem on the beach. Despite their tiny size they can give you a nasty bite. And, ants abound, so make sure you check the ground carefully before sitting down otherwise you might get bitten, and the bites can itch for days.

Sea urchins, jelly fish and fire coral should all be avoided in the water.

Note: Drinking water from the tap is perfectly safe although bottled mineral and distilled water is widely available.

HOSPITALS

There are 14 pubic and private hospitals on the island.

Kingston

**Andrews Memorial
Hospital (private)**
☎ 926-7401
**Bustamante Hospital
for Children**
☎ 926-5721

Kingston Public Hospital
☎ 922-0210
**Medical Associates
Hospital (private)**
☎ 926-1400

Nuttall Memorial Hospital (private)
☎ 926-2139
St Joseph's Hospital (private)
☎ 928-4955
University of West Indies Hospital
☎ 927-1620

Mandeville

Hargreaves Memorial Hospital (private)
☎ 962-2040
Mandeville Hospital
☎ 962-2067

Montego Bay

Cornwall Regional Hospital
☎ 952-5100

Doctor's Hospital (private)
☎ 952-1616
MoBay Hope Medical Center,
Half Moon Shopping Village
offers 24 hour emergency service

Ocho Rios

St Ann's Bay Hospital
☎ 972-0150

Port Antonio

Port Antonio Hospital
☎ 993-2646

St Thomas

Princess Margaret Hospital
☎ 982-1093/2304

HUSTLING

Hustling is almost a way of life on Jamaica. Many people need to hustle to make ends meet, others do it for fun to see how much they can get. It is impossible to go to Jamaica without being hustled, especially along the north coast, but do not feel threatened by it or get angry at it as you will get teased even more. If asked for money or offered something you do not want, decline in a firm but friendly way. Young women on holiday alone will be propositioned, sometimes outrageously, by Jamaican men. Again, if you not interested say so openly and directly, which will not cause offense.

INSURANCE

Make sure you have adequate insurance to cover all eventualities. Health care if required, is expensive, and if hiring a car, it is worth taking out extra insurance such as damage collision waiver. If you have rented a car as part of a package deal, check what insurance cover this includes, and make up any shortcomings.

LANGUAGE

The official language is English but a local patois, a combination of several languages, is widely spoken. The patois is virtually incomprehensible to visitors, but a few words are useful.

don man – an important person
queen – girlfriend
donna – woman
yeow – hello
dunza – money
yowa – come here

MEDIA

There are three daily newspapers, two morning – the Daily Gleaner, founded in 1834, and The Record -and one evening tabloid, The Star, all published in Kingston, and five Sunday newspapers. Most major US newspapers and many foreign papers and magazines are readily available. The Jamaica Broadcasting Corporation provides radio and television channels, and KLAS and Radio Jamaica also run radio stations.

MINERAL SPRINGS

There are several mineral springs of which four have bathing facilities. There are public springs at Bath in St Thomas, and Milk River in Clarendon. The Rockfort Mineral Baths, Kingston, is run by the Cement Company.

NATIONAL SYMBOLS

National Fruit: The Ackee   **National Tree:**   Mahoe
National Bird: The Doctor Bird   **National Flower:** Lignum Vitae

Sand Castle Pub, Ocho Rios

NIGHTLIFE

It is said that Kingston never closes, and there are lots of bars and nightspots. You can also find places for late night music and a drink in the other large towns, but there is little to do away from urban areas. Most of the resorts and large hotels provide their own evening entertainment with local musicians, dance groups and cabaret acts, and late night discos.

Kingston
Asylum, 24 Karat, Atlantis, Cactus, Carlos, Chasers. Country-side, Godfather's, Grizzly's, Grog Shoppe, Junkanoo Lounge, Mingles, Mirage, Peppers, Priscilla's and the Turntable.
Mandeville area
Planet Disco, Tracks Disco, 'N' Somnia and Ward 21.
Montego Bay area
Aquasol, The Brewery, Cave Disco, Coconuts Club, Disco Inferno, Hurricane, Impact Disco, Junkanoo Lounge, Margueritaville, The Native, Pier 1, Planet Xaymaka, Rhythm, Witches, Walter's Bar and Zulu's

Negril Area
Arthur's Golden Sunset, Close Encounters Disco, Compulsion, Hedonism 11 Disco, Kaiser's, MX3, Rick's Cafe and Visions
Ocho Rios area
Acropolis, Amnesia, Bill's Place, Evita's, Little Pub, Jamaica Me Krazy, Reggae Paradise, Roof Club, Shades, Silks Club and Vintage Bar
Port Antonio area
Roof Club and Shadows.

PETS

Pets are not allowed as the island is rabies-free and there are strict controls to enforce this.

PHOTOGRAPHS

The intensity of the sun can play havoc with your films, especially if photographing near water or white sand. Compensate for the brightness otherwise your photographs will come out over-exposed and wishy washy, especially if you take pictures when the sun is at its strongest. A low speed film is preferable – ASA 64 for slides, or ASA 100 for prints and underwater shots. If photographing on the beach in bright sunlight set the camera at least one stop and perhaps two below the reading from the built in light meter. The heat can actually damage film so store reels in a box or bag in the hotel fridge if there is one. Also remember to protect your camera if on the beach, as a single grain of sand is all it takes to jam your camera, and if left unprotected, it might disappear. Film is expensive and it is best to bring your own, but if you have to buy, make sure that the expiry date is still a long way off. It is also a good idea to bring with you any replacement batteries your camera might need.

It is very easy to get 'click happy' in the Caribbean, but be tactful when taking photographs. Many islanders are shy or simply fed up with being photographed, and others will insist on a small payment. You will have to decide whether the picture is worth it, but if a person declines to have their photograph taken, don't ignore this. The islanders are a warm and very hospitable people, and if you stop and spend some time finding out what they are doing, they will usually then allow you to take a photograph. Film is quite expensive and it is better to take it with you, and carry spare batteries if your camera requires them, or change them for new ones just before departure.

POST

The main post office is on the corner of King Street and Barry Street, Kingston ☎ 922-2120. There are post offices in all towns and stamps are sold in many stores, hotels and attractions. In Mango Bay, there are post offices next to Doctor Caves Beach and 1 St James Street. In Negril, the post office is on West End Road, and in Ocho Rios it is on Main Street.

PUBLIC HOLIDAYS * AND MAJOR EVENTS

January

January 1 New Year's Day *
Accompong Maroon Festival
St Elizabeth
Air Jamaica Jazz and Blues Festival
National Art Exhibition
Pantomime
Negril Sprint Triathlon
High Mountain 10k road race,
Williamsfield

February

Bob Marley Birthday Bash
Nine Miles, St Ann and Bob Marley Museum, Kingston
Chukka Cove Appleton Polo Tournament
UWI Carnival
Jamaica Marathon

March

Annual Negril Reggae Festival
Annual Red Stripe
International Polo Festival
Chukka Cove
Ash Wednesday *
Jamaica Orchid Society Annual Spring Show

April

Good Friday *
Easter Monday *
Annual Red Stripe Horse Show
Chukka Cove
Easter Craft Fair
Ocho Rios
Jamaica Carnival
Kingston, Ocho Rios and Montego Bay
Montego Bay Yacht Club Easter Regatta

May

Labour day *
Manchester Horticultural Society Show
South Coast Fishing Tournament
Black River

June

Jamaica Festival National Heroes Tribute
National Heroes Park
Jamaica Festival Performing Arts Final
Ocho Rios Jazz Festival

July

Jamaica Festival Popular Song Contest
Kingston
Manchester Golf Week
Reggae Sunsplash
Kingston
Negril Carnival
National Dance Theatre Company's Season of Dance
Kingston
Jamaica Spice Food Festival

August

Independence Day 1st Monday *
Harmong Hall Craft Fair
Ocho Rios
Hi-Pro Family Polo Tournament and International Horse Show
Chukka Cove
Portland Jamboree
Reggae Sumfest
Montego Bay

September

Falmouth Blue Marlin Tournament
Miss Jamaica World

Beauty Pageant
Kingston
Montego Bay International Marlin Tournament

October

National Heroes Day – 3rd Monday *
Fossil Open Polo Tournament
Chukka Cove
Jamaica Open Pepsi Pro Am Golf Tournament
Montego Bay
Oktoberfest
Kingston
Port Antonio International Marlin Tournament
National Mento Yard

November

Jamaica Golf Week
International Carting Week
Kingston
Royal Jamaica Yacht Club Fishing Tournament
Thanksgiving Craft Fair
Ocho Rios

December

Ikebana International Show
Kingston
JAM-AM Cup Yacht Race
Montego Bay
Johnnie Walker World Championship
Tryall Golf, Beach and Tennis Club
December 25 – Christmas Day *
December 26 – Boxing Day *

SECURITY

Sensible precautions should be taken to avoid petty pilfering which can be a problem. It makes sense like anywhere else, not to walk around wearing expensive jewelry or flashing large sums of money. Extra care needs to be taken late at night, especially away from the centers of the larger towns, where street crime occasionally occurs. If out late at night, travel by taxi or with a crowd, and don't stray into unfamiliar, badly lit areas. It is a good idea to get a street map and familiarize yourself with it, learning the best way back to your hotel, not necessarily the quickest. Don't leave valuable items in unattended vehicles, or on the beach if going swimming.

Don't carry around your passport, traveler's checks or all your money. Keep them secure in your room or in a hotel safety deposit box. It is also a good idea to have photocopies of the information page of your passport, your air ticket and holiday insurance policy. All will help greatly if the originals are lost. Most hotels have their own security staff, but care should also be taken with valuables when by the pool and on the beach.

As with most tourist destinations, you might be pestered by touts trying to sell tours, souvenirs and even drugs, or by young people begging. A firm 'no' or 'not interested', is normally enough to persuade them to leave you alone.

SHOPPING

Shops and boutiques of all kinds can be found on the island selling a huge range of goods. There are duty-free shops and designer boutiques, crafts markets and top-name salons, as well as street vendors and roadside stands, and remember that haggling over the price is all part of the fun.

Kingston, Montego Bay and Ocho Rios have a number of shopping centers and malls. Best buys include local woodwork, straw weaving, beads and embroidery from the Craft Market. Gold, silver, jewelry, china, crystal and electronic goods from in-bond stores, clothing, rum, Blue Mountain coffee and perfumes are all good buys. Shops are open from Monday to Saturday although some close on Wednesday or Thursday afternoon.

If self-catering best buys are fresh fruit and vegetables, bread, freshly caught fish. Young coconuts provide refreshing drinks and sugar cane sticks are very nutritious.

TAXES

There is a 15% Government tax on accommodation, in addition to any service charge which may be added.

Right: Jamaica Express Airways

Below: Getting around the island is cheap and easy using the regular bus service

TELEPHONES AND COMMUNICATIONS

There are pay phones but they might not always be working. For local calls you need two ten cent coins which are inserted when the person you are calling answers, for long distance and international calls it is better to call collect rather than juggle with all the coins needed. For local calls dial the 7-digit number, for long distance island calls, prefix the 7-digit number with a 0. For directory inquiries dial 114, for the international operator dial 113. In most hotels, calls have to be placed through the operator for which a charge is made, plus a surcharge for long distance and international calls. The international dialing code for Jamaica is 876, and from the US it is a long distance call – dial 1-876 and then the 7-digit number. From the UK dial 001-876 and then the local number.

TIME

Jamaica observes Eastern Standard Time, the same as New York, which is five hours behind GMT, so when it is noon in London it is 7am in Kingston. Daylight Saving Time is not observed so during the summer months, Jamaica is one hour behind New York and four hours ahead of London.

TIPPING

It is customary to tip about 15% in restaurants and add the same to taxi fares. Some hotels and restaurants add a 15% service charge to bills, so check to ensure you do not pay twice. Tip porters about $1 for each large piece of luggage carried, and leave room maids about $1 for each night's accommodation.

TOURIST OFFICES

There are tourist information offices at:

Black River
Hendriks Building, 2 High Street, Black River, St Elizabeth
☎ 965-2074
Kingston
2 St Lucia Avenue, PO Box 360, Kingston 5
☎ 929-9200
**Norman Manley
International Airport**
☎ 924-8024
Montego Bay
Cornwall Beach, PO Box 67, Montego Bay
☎ 952-4425

Sangster International Airport
☎ 952-2462
Negril
Coral Seas Plaza
☎ 957-4243
Ocho Rios
Ocean Village Shopping Centre, PO Box 240, Ocho Rios
☎ 974-2582
Port Antonio
City Centre Plaza, PO Box 151, Port Antonio
☎ 993-3051

There are Jamaica Tourist Board offices abroad in:

United States

300 West Wieuca Road NE
Suite 100-A, Atlanta GA 30342
☎ 404 250-9971
21 Merchants Row
5th floor, Boston MA 02109
☎ 617 248-5811
500 North Michigan Avenue
Suite 1030, Chicago Il 60611
☎ 312 527-1296
8214 Westchester
Suite 500, Dallas TX 75225
☎ 214 361-8778
26400 Lahser Road
Suite 114-A, Southfield,
Detroit MI 48034
☎ 313 948-9557
3440 Wilshire Boulevard
Suite 805, Los Angeles
CA 90010
☎ 213 384-1123

1320 South Dixie Highway
Suite 1101, Coral Gables,
Miami Fl 33146
☎ 305 665-0557
801 Second Avenue
20th floor, New York NY 10017
☎ 212 856-9727
1315 Walnut Street
Suite 1505, Philadelphia
PA 19107
☎ 215 545-1061

Canada

1 Eglinton Avenue East
Suite 616, Toronto,
Ontario M4P 3A1
☎ 416 482-7850

UK

1-2 Prince Consort Road
London SW7 2BZ
☎ 0207-224-0505

TRAVEL AROUND THE ISLAND

Mini-buses and shared taxis operate around the island and are a cheap and fun way to travel. Mini buses have their own routes and only leave when the drivers think there are enough passengers. They can get very crowded and are always noisy. The journey is slow because of frequent stops, but it is a great chance to get to meet the islanders. Mini-buses are best used for comparatively short journeys, because you can waste several hours traveling from Kingston to Montego Bay. Shared taxis are quicker because they make fewer stops, and are cost effective if there are enough of you.

Public buses operate throughout Kingston and there are also public passenger services around the island connecting villages, towns and cities. They usually have indicator boards showing where they are going, but it is always advisable to ask in case the driver has not changed the sign! The buses are slow and at peak times can be crowded with standing room only. In towns they only stop at bus stops, but can be waved down in country areas. Traveling by bus from Kingston to Montego can take several hours, and traveling to other destinations may involve delays changing from one bus to another. For instance, if you are traveling from Montego Bay to Port Antonio, you have to change four times.

Fact File

Bus Stations:

Montego Bay – Barnett Street
Ocho Rios – opposite the Farmers' Market
Port Antonio – Foreshore Road
Negril – next to the police station

Taxis:

Taxis have the letters PPV (Public Passenger Vehicle) on their red registration plates and should be metered, although many are not. JUTA taxis have fixed fares that should be displayed. It is always advisable, however, to agree the fare before getting in, especially when first arriving and tired after a long flight. Do not take rides in unlicensed non-PPV taxis as these may not be insured. You will get hustled by the taxi drivers at the airport but taxi drivers make excellent tour guides and can be hired for sightseeing tours but always agree the price before setting off. Expect to pay about J$500-550 an hour for sightseeing tours, which is very reasonable if being split several ways.

By rail:

The railroad was introduced in 1845 and the line runs from Kingston north west via Spanish Town, Williamsfield (outside Mandeville) and Maggotty to Montego Bay. There were two trains a day from Kingston to Montego Bay and back and the journey took almost six hours offering incredible scenery en route. Unfortunately, the service closed down in1995 but it is hoped to re-open it.

By air:

There are domestic airports at Tinson Pen, close to Kingston's waterfront, Negril, Boscobel, Ocho Rios and Ken Jones airport at Port Antonio, and a number of private air strips. Domestic airports are served by Air Jamaica Express, Trans Jamaica Airlines, Air SuperClub and Tropical Airlines. Helitours Jamaica also offers spectacular tours of the island. Flying around the island is very good value, and return tickets are considerably cheaper than two singles.

WEDDINGS

Many people choose to marry in Jamaica and the following requirements have to be met. Couples have to have been resident for at least 24 hours before being married. They can apply in advance for a marriage license (JA$200) and must provide proof of citizenship (a certified copy of birth certificate), parent's written consent if under the age of 18, proof of divorce if applicable, and a copy of death certificate for widow or widower. A blood test is not required.

Applications must be made to the Ministry of National Security and Justice, 12 Ocean Boulevard, Kingston ☎ 922-0080. The office is open between 8.30am and 5pm Monday to Thursday and 8.30am to 4pm on Friday. Many hotels have wedding consultants who will make all the necessary arrangements. There are also a number of non-denominational marriage registrars who will conduct the ceremony for a fee.

A typical wedding ceremony on the beach front

INDEX

LANDMARK
VISITORS GUIDES

US & British VI*
ISBN: 1 901522 03 2
256pp,
UK £11.95 US $15.95

Antigua & Barbuda*
ISBN: 1 901522 02 4
96pp,
UK £5.95 US $12.95

Bermuda*
ISBN: 1 901522 07 5
160pp,
UK £7.95 US $12.95

Barbados*
ISBN: 1 901522 32 6
144pp,
UK £6.95 US $12.95

St Lucia*
ISBN: 1 901522 8
144pp,
UK £6.95 US $13

Pack
2 months
into
2 weeks
with your

Landmark
Visitors
Guides

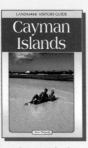

Cayman Islands*
ISBN: 1 901522 33 4
144pp
UK £6.95 US $12.95

Orlando*
ISBN: 1 901522 22 9
256pp,
UK £9.95 US $15.95

Florida: Gulf Coast*
ISBN: 1 901522 01 6
160pp
UK £7.95 US $12.95

Florida: The Key
ISBN: 1 901522 2
160pp,
UK £7.95 US $12

Dominican Republic*
ISBN: 1 901522 08 3
160pp,
UK £7.95 US $12.95

Gran Canaria*
ISBN: 1 901522 19 9
160pp
UK £7.95 US $12.95

Tenerife
ISBN: 1 901522 17 2
160pp,
UK £7.95

North Cyprus
ISBN: 1 901522 51 2
192pp
UK £8.95

Madeira
ISBN: 1 901522
192pp,
UK £8.95

To order send a cheque (check)/Visa/MasterCard details to: **Landmark Publishing**,
Waterloo House, 12 Compton, Ashbourne, Derbyshire DE6 IDA England
Tel: 01335 347349 Fax: 01335 347303 e-mail: landmark@clara.net
web site: www.landmarkpublishing.co.uk

* In USA order from **Hunter Publishing**
130 Campus Drive, Edison NJ 08818, Tel (732) 225 1900 or (800) 255 0343
Fax: (732) 417 0482 www.hunterpublishing.com

Provence*
N: 1 901522 45 8
240pp,
£10.95 US $17.95

Côte d'Azur*
ISBN: 1 901522 29 6
144pp,
UK £6.95 US $13.95

Dordogne
ISBN: 1 901522 67 9
176pp,
UK £9.95

Vendée
ISBN: 1 901522 76 X
160pp,
UK £7.95

Languedoc
ISBN: 1 901522 79 2
144pp,
UK £6.95

Bruges*
N: 1 901522 66 0
96pp,
£5.95 US $10.95

Ticino
ISBN: 1 901522 74 1
192pp
UK £8.95

Italian Lakes*
ISBN: 1 901522 11 3
240pp,
UK £10.95 US $15.95

Riga*
ISBN: 1 901522 59 8
160pp,
UK £7.95

Cracow
ISBN: 1 901522 54 7
160pp,
UK £7.95

Iceland*
N: 1 901522 68 7
192pp,
12.95 US $17.95

New Zealand*
ISBN: 1 901522 36 9
320pp
UK £12.95 US $18.95

Sri Lanka
ISBN: 1 901522 37 7
192pp,
UK £9.95

India: Kerala
ISBN: 1 901522 16 4
256pp,
UK £10.99

India: Goa
ISBN: 1 901522 23 7
160pp,
UK £7.95

Prices subject to alteration from time to time

Published in the UK by
Landmark Publishing Ltd,
Waterloo House, 12 Compton, Ashbourne, Derbyshire DE6 1DA England
Tel: (01335) 347349 Fax: (01335) 347303
e-mail: sales@landmarkpublishing.co.uk
website: landmarkpublishing.co.uk

Published in the USA by
Hunter Publishing Inc,
130 Campus Drive, Edison NJ 08818
Tel: (732) 225 1900, (800) 255 0343 Fax: (732) 417 0482
website: www.hunterpublishing.com

ISBN 1 901 522 31 8
© **Don Philpott**

British Library Cataloguing in Publication Data: a catalogue record for this
book is available from the British Library.

Print: Gutenberg Press Ltd, Malta
Cartography: Mark Titterton
Design: Mark Titterton

Front cover: Negril, parm fringed beach
Back cover, top: Harmony Hall, Och Rios
Back cover, bottom: Ocho Rios

Picture Credits
**All photography supplied by the author and The Jamaican Tourist
Board except the following: Photobank** Front cover and page 3